Let's STOP Beating Around the BUSH

Let's STOP Beating Around the BUSH

More POLITICAL SUBVERSION from

JIM HIGHTOWER

The NEW YORK TIMES bestselling author of
THIEVES IN HIGH PLACES

VIKING

VIKING
Published by the Penguin Group
Penguin Group (USA) Inc., 375 Hudson Street, New York, New York 10014, U.S.A.
Penguin Books Ltd, 80 Strand, London WC2R 0RL, England
Penguin Books Australia Ltd, 250 Camberwell Road, Camberwell, Victoria 3124, Australia
Penguin Books Canada Ltd, 10 Alcorn Avenue, Toronto, Ontario, Canada M4V 3B2
Penguin Books India (P) Ltd, 11 Community Centre, Panchsheel Park,
    New Delhi – 110 017, India
Penguin Group (NZ), Cnr Airborne and Rosedale Roads, Albany, Auckland 1310,
    New Zealand
Penguin Books (South Africa) (Pty) Ltd, 24 Sturdee Avenue, Rosebank, Johannesburg 2196,
    South Africa

Penguin Books Ltd, Registered Offices:
80 Strand, London WC2R 0RL, England

First published in 2004 by Viking Penguin,
a member of Penguin Group (USA) Inc.

10   9   8   7   6   5   4   3   2   1

Some of the selections in this book first appeared in *The Hightower Lowdown* or originated
as the author's radio commentaries and were later adapted for publication in various peri-
odicals. "Why Libraries Matter" first appeared in *American Libraries* magazine.

An excerpt from the liner notes for the album "Triage" by David Baerwald is reprinted by
permission of David Baerwald.

LIBRARY OF CONGRESS CATALOGING-IN-PUBLICATION DATA IS AVAILABLE

0-670-03354-5

This book is printed on acid-free paper. ∞

Printed in the United States of America
Designed by Carla Bolte • Set in Adobe Garamond with Bauer Bodini

To my godchild,

ISABELLA MARGUERIE ABATE

What's the use of writing

if you can't piss someone off.

ACKNOWLEDGMENTS

Thank you, *Susan DeMarco*—thank you to the nth power for all the creativity you put into this, from helping to conceptualize the book to taking your ever sharp editing pencil to it, fixing what I had thought was absolutely sparkling prose. You're right: Less is more, even when it hurts (but don't hold me to that in my next book).

Thanks to my niece, *Lisa Abate* (yes, my books are like a family-owned trattoria, where we all chip in to make the puttanesca sauce), whose zippy "Six Perfectly Good Reasons" frames the chapters and, hard as it is to imagine, who made an election-year book fun—at least to us.

In my small office in Austin, thanks, thanks, thanks to *Laura Ehrlich* and *Sean Doles*. They are the heart and soul, sweat and sanity of my Saddle-Burr Productions, churning out a torrent of well-researched information, creative ideas, and old-fashioned hard work.

Short of giving each reader a beer, I figured that the best thing I could do to lighten the potential load of this work was to offer diversions in the form of art and puzzles. *Matt Wuerker* is a gem of a political cartoonist, whom I've had the privilege of knowing and working with for five years at *The Hightower Lowdown,* my monthly newsletter. Even if you don't read this book, skip through to his illustrations in each of the six chapters, and you'll get the idea of whatever it is I'm trying to say. Also, to punctuate my points, each chapter offers a Bush puzzle or quiz for your amusement, and I thank my Austin pal and fellow writer *Mary Willis* for her puzzle-meistering.

Praise be also to *Adrian Zackheim,* my hardy editor and friend, who has weathered four books with me now. I know he's been confronted more than once by higher-ups asking: "Tell us again why we're publishing this guy?" Thank you. And also to my agent, *Rafe Sagalyn,* who when push comes to shove, will.

Finally, thanks to all the great folks working to produce *The Hightower Lowdown* as well as my daily radio commentaries and newspaper columns. Much of the material in this book is drawn from material I wrote for these outlets in the past couple of years.

Oh, and one more thank-you: Thanks, George W, Cheney, Rummy, Ashcroft, Rove, and the rest of the Bushite menagerie. I surely could not have done this without you. Now, please go away, so I don't have to do this again.

CONTENTS

BUSH...AGAIN?

Six Perfectly Good Reasons to Elect George W. Bush

2: CHEAP UNDERWEAR, BUB   39

George W Does the Economy

3: ONE WORD, BUCKO: YUM-YUM-YUM! 77

George W Does Food

4: YOU'LL NEVER HAVE TO FEEL ALONE AGAIN, MY FRIEND 115

George W Does Liberty

5: RUGGED INDIVIDUALISM, COMPADRE 155

George W Does the Common Good

INTRODUCTION

"You've got to take the bull by the teeth."
—movie mogul Samuel Goldwyn

Whoa, Sam, you could lose a hand doing that! Yet here I am foolishly practicing Goldwyn's malapropism, reaching right into the maw of the Bush White House to try throwing this raging bull to the ground.

Why? Because the Bushites are—let me put this as politely as I can—NUTS! Bull-goose-loopy, ideological freaks, whose snorting rampages pose a threat to us all and to all we hold dear.

Oh, I can hear you thinking [**Reader's Alert:** It's true, I have uncanny ears]: *Surely he doesn't mean* loopy. *While the Bushites might be unusually robust, aggressive even, in the pursuit of their agenda, they are still within the bounds of America's mainstream political thought . . . right? It's not like they're, you know, EXTREMISTS who would try to superimpose their own Orwellian, Strangelovian, AynRandian, JerryFallwellian ideology over America's good ol' egalitarian ideals . . . right? I mean, these are rational people who just happen to be a little to the right . . . right?*

No. They're insane. They're zealots totally dedicated to implementing their plutocratic, autocratic, militaristic, and imperialistic vision of America—and it's time we stopped beating around the bush about it.

How crazy are they? Consider these symptoms: Rumsfeld— scowling, barking, and thrusting out his chest—sees weapons of mass destruction that are not there; George himself constantly hears voices in his head telling him to "cut rich people's taxes . . . again"; Ashcroft lunges from place to place, frenetically searching for more ways to "protect" our freedom by (follow the bouncing logic here) throttling our freedoms; and Cheney, with that fiendish grin always slashed across his face, insists that God created earth so oil companies would have something to plunder.

These people must be stopped and taken away to a very quiet, soothing place where they can no longer do harm. Think about it. In four short years, they have:

- heisted $1.3 trillion from our public treasury and doled it out to their richest campaign backers;
- defoliated our environmental protections;
- launched a class war not only against the poor but against the middle class as well;
- taken a Weedwacker to our Bill of Rights;
- sought to castrate labor unions;
- turned a $240 billion budget surplus into a $520 billion debt;
- attempted to privatize everything from the Park Service to Social Security;
- and hurled our nation into a maniacal, messianic, testosterone-driven global war to make the world safe for Halliburton.

Imagine what they'd be doing if they'd actually won the election!

Now imagine what they *will* be doing if they win this one . . . or if they Supreme-Court it again.

Unbelievable is a word usually reserved for breathtaking circus acts or the kind of astonishing oddities found in *Ripley's Believe It or Not,* but it has now become the defining term for the madness of King George the W. As I've crisscrossed America since the Bushites took power, person after person has come forward—mouth agape, head shaking, eyes wide—with yet another horror story of the mind-boggling arrogance and downright weirdness of this bunch. And every one of their stories is punctuated with "Unbelievable!"

Bush & Company have made the bizarre commonplace. So common that whenever there's another White House announcement of some action they've either taken or proposed, people instinctively cringe: "Oh no, here it comes again." What "it" is doesn't matter, for people know it's going to be yet another awful step backward, another dollop of unfathomable ideological excess, and another wallop for the rest of us.

When I say "people" cringe, I don't merely mean yellow-dog Democrats, but also political switch-hitters, Libertarians, nonvoters, none-of-the-abovers, and—grab your stuffed elephant, George!—*Republicans*. Not only are lots of mainstream, moderate, Rockefeller Republicans appalled by Boy Bush's wacked-out right-wing policies, but so are many Barry Goldwater conservatives. They don't think of the USA Patriot Act, profligate federal spending, unlimited war on whomever, the relentless assault on local sovereignty, the proliferation of executive secrecy, unfettered corporate welfare, et cetera, et cetera, as being "conservative."

A middle-aged lady came up to me in a coffee shop this spring and said, "I don't want to bother you, but I want to say that I'm a lifelong Republican who thought I was a good conservative. But I didn't know what a lefty I must be until these people came into power. Who the hell are they?"

Nutballs, that's who. Way beyond the fringe.

However, I do realize a that number of people are die-hard Bushites, sincerely believing W to be just a regular, pretzel-eating, hail-fellow-well-met who happens to be totally convinced that his view of the world is the absolute right view—a guy (and commander-in-chief) willing to use the full force of the presidency of the United States to muscle that view into national policy, undeterred by common sense or even facts. Aggressive leadership, they call it, and bully for George!

Well, in the interest of spirited discourse, I feel honor-bound to recognize that enthusiasm. So I've called on a longtime personal buddy—a particularly proud Bushite, but one who wishes to remain anonymous in my book—to lead each chapter with his insights into why Glorious George is the best White House occupant since McKinley.

After all, George W certainly is a likable son-of-a-Bush—all the more so if he's putting money in your corporate pockets. Therefore, giving credit where credit is due, I've organized this book in a contrarian fashion, offering "Six Perfectly Good Reasons to Elect George W. Bush." Fair is fair.

1

Global Warming!

☞ *Thanks to Bush's pollution policies, if you buy some cheap land in Appalachia today, by the time you're ready to retire, it'll be prime oceanfront property.*

*T*hink about it: If Bush is elected, you'll soon be able to surf in Asheville, go beachcombing in Austin, and have clambakes on the shores of Phoenix. What's not to like about that? Besides, I've been to Boston, Chicago, Minneapolis, Missoula, and other northern climes in the winter months, and let me tell you—you people could use some warming up!

Sure, global warming is melting the polar ice caps, but let me ask a basic question here: Do we really need all that ice? Hello! It's 2004—you have air-conditioning, and your fridge comes with an icemaker, for God's sake.

And stop it already with the constant whining about the so-called ozone hole at the north and south poles. Don't you listen to Rush Limbaugh? It's a hoax, folks! Ain't happening. Nothing but a ploy by enviro-wacko groups to scare people into sending them money. But even if it is happening—SO FRIGGING WHAT! You don't have to go to the Arctic, do you? It's a matter of taking personal responsibility.

Sure, sure, there are Eskimos and some wilderness weirdos who choose to live up there, but there's no need to get government involved and bring America's mighty economic machine to a grinding halt just because a few of them are worried about sunburn and a little skin cancer. Instead of seeing the ozone hole as an environmental problem, let's recognize it for what it is: an economic opportunity for the sunscreen industry. All the sunscreen boys need from Washington is a tax break, a marketing subsidy, and an exemption from any legal liability, then—whoa, Nellie—stand back and watch 'em go! They'll slather the Arctic in a sea of sunscreen, boost our economy, create jobs, extend democracy to every hamlet on earth, help prevent terrorism, and lift all boats. It's called "free enterprise," bubba.

And that right there is your difference between George W and the latte-sipping, socialist-hugging Democrat crowd. George trusts the free market to do what's best for us—while, deep in their hearts, that other crowd can't stand the thought that you might get some oceanfront property out of the deal if we just let Bush and the corporations work their magic.

M. WUERKER

GEORGE W DOES THE ENVIRONMENT

Sigh. I miss the good ol' days of environmental protection. Under Nixon, for example.

"*Nixon!!?* You been putting jimsonweed in your cereal again, Hightower?"

Well, ethically and politically, Tricky Dick definitely was a piece of sleaze, but he actually had a tidy streak in him when it came to cleaning up pollution. Whether or not his motives were pure or purely political, Nixon's the guy who signed the bills creating the EPA, OSHA, the Clean Air Act, and the Clean Water Act. See, being a Republican president doesn't *require* you to whore for polluters and plunderers.

For that matter, give me Reagan. Yes, I know Ronnie was clueless, dottily declaring at one point that "Trees cause more pollution than automobiles." And yes, I know that he put James "Chainsaw" Watt in charge of our nation's natural resources—a dangerous joker who approached his governmental stewardship with an airheaded mix of laissez-faire corporatism and religious extremism, leading him to utter such blinding insights as, "We don't have to protect the environment, the Second Coming is at hand." But I also know that, back then, we used to think: "It can't get any worse than this."

Welcome to the regime of George W. Twenty years later, we're looking back wistfully, realizing that the bumbling Reaganauts were practically Earth Firsters compared to the skilled Scorched Earthers now in charge. For someone named for a plant, Bush has shown an astonishing hostility to nature. Bush, Cheney & Company never met a polluter too filthy to hug, especially if the *abrazo* comes with a generous campaign check.

The breadth of their all-out assault on our air, water, and all things natural is breathtaking . . . literally! Take Bush's Clear Skies initiative. Despite its spiffy name, it twists Nixon's Clean Air Act inside out, allowing electric companies, chemical plants, oil refineries, and other inveterate spewers of toxics to goose up their profits by gleefully pumping an additional *forty-two tons* of their industrial poisons into our air (and lungs) each year. This is a regulatory favor that the National Academy of Sciences calculates will, in turn, cause an extra thirty thousand American deaths each year.

[Bulletin: We break our narrative here to bring you this important background report on Bush's internal policy operations. It's never been revealed before, but reliable sources have informed this intrepid reporter that somewhere deep in the sub-sub-sub-basement of the White House, possibly bunkered with Dick Cheney, is a thin, yellow-skinned, shifty-eyed former advertising executive for the tobacco industry who goes only by his code name, Flaco. Reportedly subsisting on nothing but Twinkies, instant coffee, and unfiltered cigarettes, Flaco is the operative accountable for the policy slogans that Karl Rove feeds to the media. In addition to "Clear Skies," Flaco's recent work includes "Healthy Forests," a convoluted Bush plan that allows the timber boys to grow their profits by cutting down perfectly healthy and extremely profitable old-growth trees from our national forests. Inside sources, speaking on condition of anonymity, tell us that Flaco cackles like an insane hen each time he comes up with another "Clear Skies" or "Healthy Forests" to slap onto a Bush policy that does the exact opposite of what the slogan advertises. We're also informed that whenever Flaco's cackle reverberates from the depths, the president's face lights up with childlike joy. **Now back to the narrative in progress.]**

Remember those Chinese snakehead fish that invaded some ponds in suburban Washington in 2002? The snakehead is an almost unnatural species, terrifying to behold. More than three feet long, this invasive and aggressive Asian native has a large mouth,

DIRTY MONEY

In 2000, Bush had 241 "Pioneers"—corporate representatives who each raised $100,000 or more for his election. Nearly a fourth of them represented polluter interests, including the National Mining Association, the lobbying front for coal companies. Once in office, Bush promptly began rolling out favors, giving them billions of dollars' worth of special breaks on mine safety, environmental protections, waste disposal, etc. After only a year of Bush gifts, William Raney, head honcho of the West Virginia Coal Association, was giddy as he told a gathering of 150 coal barons:

"You did everything you could to elect a Republican president. You are already seeing in his actions the payback!"

A grateful National Association of Mining is now signed up as an enthusiastic Bush "Ranger," promising to raise $200,000 or more this time around.

big teeth, predatory instincts, and a voracious appetite. It can clear a pond of all other fish in a hurry. Then—get this—it's capable of living out of water for several days, slithering on its belly and fins across land to find another pond to devour. Along the way, the snakehead indiscriminately eats any small animals it encounters. With no natural predators, it literally can upset the balance of nature, and it will continue its onslaught unless someone kills it.

The Bush administration is the Chinese snakehead of environmental politics. It is aggressively devouring America's antipollution protections and upsetting the balance of power so its corporate backers can work their will.

There's never been a presidency like this, so totally, unabashedly, and aggressively corporate, despite not having won a majority of the people's vote, much less any kind of mandate to upend three decades of environmental progress.

In only three short years, the Bushites have launched an executive, judicial, legislative, and PR assault to undermine and kill more than two hundred of our country's most basic environmental safeguards. They have rolled back everything from rules that protect our children from lead poisoning to rules for the protection of that thin ozone layer, which is all that stands between us and the sun's rays that otherwise would fry us human types (including Republicans!) in our own juices and parch our little planet. Never has a president gone to such extremes to give away so much in such a short time.

It started on Day One of Bush II. As George W was being inaugurated, his new chief of staff, Andy Card (previously the chief Washington lobbyist for General Motors), quietly issued a White House moratorium on all enviro regulations recently enacted by the Clinton administration, asserting that these rules were "unfair" to the polluters. Thus was hung a big red banner on the White House, proclaiming that the presidency was under new management, now offering 24/7 drive-through service for oil, auto, timber, mining, agribusiness, nuclear, chemical, developer, and other polluter interests that had financed the Bush-Cheney ascension to power.

The corporate media, especially the television networks (owned by such conglomerate polluters as General Electric and Disney), have provided only sporadic coverage to this serial mugging of the environment. Each part of the thuggery is astonishing, but the whole adds up to what should be treated as a premeditated capital crime against our people and against nature itself. We shouldn't merely be campaigning against them, we should be hunting them down with dogs.

Bush Gets Hot

George W is a global kind of guy—he's a big promoter of corporate globalization, and, of course, he's launched his unlimited global war on terrorism. But mention "global warming" to him, and he turns into a flat-earth parochialist, flailing his arms, getting all red-faced, and sputtering and spewing that global warming is a trick, not really happening, and if it *is* happening it's not the fault of big industry, and if it *is* their fault there's nothing we're gonna do about it, so go fly a kite, you environmental weenies!

Never mind that the vast majority of scientists agree that global warming is all too real of a threat, and that 72 percent of Americans think we need to take immediate steps to deal with this threat. That's a lot of weenies, George.

What counts for Bush, however, are not the millions of concerned Americans but the millions of campaign dollars put in his pockets by the corporate polluters causing the warming. In the 2000 election, he was the number one recipient of their campaign cash, and in turn, he has put dozens of energy executives, lobbyists, and consultants in key positions to oversee energy policy.

How embarrassing, then, that the scientists in George's own Environmental Protection Agency (EPA) issued a report concluding that (1) global warming is happening, (2) it's mostly caused by fossil fuel pollution, and (3) it will have disastrous global consequences if we don't act promptly to stop it. But rather than act—or even act embarrassed—Bush dismissed the scientific report with a wave of his hand, saying scornfully, "I read the report put out by the bureaucracy."

But guess what? He never actually read it! His media flack later admitted that this is true, curtly informing the media that "Whenever presidents say they read it, you can read that to be he was briefed."

Oh, thank you for clearing up the fibbery. But in George's case, we know we can read that to mean he was *bought*—no briefing necessary.

This leaves us to ponder one of earth's most important environmental questions: How deeply can George W stick his head into the Arctic tundra before having to admit that, yes, global warming just might be a wee bit of a problem for us?

The thin layer of ozone that encapsulates our globe is kind of important, since without it, the sun . . . how shall I put this? . . . will burn us to a crisp, wiping out all life on earth. Unfortunately, pollution from such things as our oil-guzzling cars is eating away this natural and essential sunscreen, causing everything from more cancer to global warming.

This is "the basic" enviro issue facing everyone, since if we don't deal with it, we won't be around to worry about any of the others.

The Bushites, however, goaded by ozone-depleting fat cats, are pretending that this isn't happening, therefore there's no need to stop the pollution causing it. But nature has a way of rudely pricking political

---

HOCUS-POCUS

Did you know that being president conveys magical powers? Don't like an environmental law? *Poof*—you can just disappear it!

The primary cause of global warming is CO_2—carbon dioxide emissions from auto tailpipes and electric power plants. But industry doesn't want to pay for the technology that will curb CO_2. So the Bushites simply shouted "Abracadabra!"—and carbon dioxide magically disappeared as a pollutant. Oh, it's still there, of course, still polluting, but Bush's environmental wrecking crew simply *redefined* CO_2 in a way that, they claim, exempts it from regulation under our Clean Air Act.

delusions with stark reality. Specifically, the frozen Arctic tundra it-self is now thawing due to global warming.

This is a problem for Bush, not because it pokes an embarrass-ing hole in his It's-Not-Happening posture (after all, Bush has never let reality interfere with ideology). Rather, the thawing tun-dra is a political problem because it's interfering with the oil giants that are drilling in Alaska. Yes—oh, cruel irony—the very industry claiming that global warming doesn't exist is now stuck in it!

An Alaskan regulation allows heavy drilling equipment on the fragile tundra only when it is frozen solid a foot deep and covered by at least six inches of snow. Thirty years ago, these wintery condi-tions existed two hundred days a year, but global warming has now shrunk this window of opportunity by half—too short a period for profitable oil drilling.

But the Bushites are remaining consistently delusional. Rather than facing up to the cause of the thawing, they want to allow the industry to drill even when the tundra is not frozen, thus produc-ing more oil to cause more global warming.

Making Government Listen

For a civics lesson on how government works in this modern age, look no further than the example of Southern Company.

Southern, a giant electric power corporation based in Atlanta, Georgia, had an idea that it wanted to convey to our national pol-icy makers. Like any citizen wanting to have its voice heard, South-ern began by introducing itself properly to those in charge. How? By becoming a major campaign contributor.

In 2000, the company gave over $500,000 to George W and other Republican candidates.

Thus, the doors of power swung open, and the utility's execu-tives were allowed to enter, getting seven separate meetings in early 2001 with Dick Cheney's secret task force that was writing Bush's new energy policy. The particular idea that the civic-minded company brought to our governmental leaders is that utilities like it should not be punished for pumping vast amounts of carbon dioxide and other toxins into the public's air.

To amplify its voice, Southern followed the time-honored democratic process: It hired a well-connected Washington lobbyist—Haley Barbour, former chairman of the Republican Party. On May 17 of that year, Bush's energy plan was released, and lo, it contained Southern's idea. See, govenment *does* listen—and responds—when properly approached.

"Just because somebody makes a campaign contribution doesn't mean that they should be denied the opportunity to express their views to government."

—Dick Cheney, 2001

But to make modern government work most efficiently for you, appropriate follow-through is important—so, note that only five days after Southern got its idea endorsed, the company and Barbour gave $350,000 to the GOP.

This money helped with yet another idea Southern had. It wanted EPA prosecutors to ignore a series of its violations of our nation's clean-air laws. Again, Haley Barbour spoke on Southern's behalf, and government once again responded fully, with the White House forcing the prosecution to drop the charges.

Not everyone, however, appreciated such smooth efficiency. Eric Schaeffer, EPA's chief of enforcement, was so disgusted that he resigned after Southern's power play, saying: "With the Bush administration . . . if you've got a good lobbyist, you can just buy your way out of trouble."

Mountain Massacre

If you've ever driven through the heart of West Virginia, you know how breathtakingly beautiful its mountains are.

Even more breathtaking, however, is the push by George W's environmental wranglers to rig both the Clean Water Act and our nation's mining laws. Why? So giant coal companies **[Warning:** Take a deep breath before you read this**]** literally can dynamite off the tops of these mountains. The coal giants delicately call this "mountaintop removal," and it's so dastardly, so grotesque, so exasperatingly stupid as to leave anyone who sees it whopper-jawed.

The story gets uglier. Having blasted off the top third or so of a mountain—along with its forests and animals—the coal companies then bulldoze the rubble (which used to be the mountaintop) into the valleys and streams below, burying them hundreds of feet deep with what the companies call "spoil."

Why this barbarous assault? Because "mountaintop massacre," as locals call it, is a dirt-cheap way for greedheaded coal barons to get at the coal down in the mountains. Luckily, we had developed regulations that restricted such avaricious sledgehammering, but that was B.B.—Before Bush. The industry had pumped a coal-train full of cash into Bush, and it even got its top lobbyist, Steven Griles, installed as George W's boss of mining rules.

So Griles and others promptly rewrote the Clean Water Act in 2002 to legalize the burying of streams, and now they're proposing a change that will effectively eliminate the only rule that still limits mountaintop removal. With a straight face, they assert that they're

❝*In the state of West Virginia, we have a need for level land.***❞**

—Former senator Jennings Randolph, explaining the logic of shearing off mountaintops

merely trying to "clarify" existing regulations and "reduce regulatory uncertainty."

Yeah, if they get their way, it'll be a certainty that 2,200 square miles of West Virginia's venerable mountains and forests will be destroyed, and it'll be clear that another 1,000 miles of mountain streams will be buried.

Bush's "Clean Coal" Boondoggle

Even George W. Bush acknowledges that he's not the brightest porch light on the block, but he seems to turn especially dim when it comes to energy policy.

W says he wants to encourage a clean energy future for us. Does that mean solar, wind, conservation, and other nonpolluting sources of power? Are you kidding? He and his sidekick Dick Cheney think all that stuff is a bunch of frou-frou, and his budget cuts back on these programs. Instead, he's thinking coal. Only a Texas oil guy could take a whiff of a lump of coal and think, ahhh . . . fresh air. Coal, of course, is about the filthiest fuel we have, but George is putting his money (actually our money) behind an oxymoron called "clean-coal technology."

Coal is to clean energy what a Twinkie is to health food. Yet for the past fifteen years, industry lobbyists have squeezed billions of dollars out of us taxpayers to subsidize utilities that build these clean-coal power plants that are only slightly less filthy than the old conventional belchers. This has been a boondoggle and a PR sham that pays utilities to build more dirty plants while claiming to be coming clean. These so-called clean-coal plants spew out ten times more smog-causing pollutants and twice as many global-warming chemicals as do utilities using natural gas.

Bush's energy plan, however, backs coal over natural gas—his bill triples the industry's subsidy, providing $5.5 billion to encourage the use of coal to generate electricity. As a result, since George has been in the White House, gleeful utility executives have announced that they will build twenty-four new coal-fired plants across the country. The result for us will be dirtier air, more health problems, increased global warming, and more acid rain.

Yet George is the same guy who tells us that government should not promote the development and use of alternative energy because he trusts the "free market" to decide which energy sources are best.

The Ever-Loopy Synfuels Loophole

Old loopholes never die—they just get loopier and loopier.

One such is a special tax break gouged into federal law back in 1980 by corporate lobbyists. In response to the energy crisis of the time, this loophole was ostensibly created to give companies an incentive to devise marketable alternatives to imported oil. But all it has really done is give companies an excuse to dodge paying the taxes they owe Uncle Sam.

The loophole is the "synfuels" tax credit for companies that reprocess coal to create new synthetic fuels. But the law's provisions are so vague that corporations have been able to claim the tax break even if their reprocessing doesn't work, doesn't reduce our dependence on oil, actually uses oil products in the so-called reprocessing, is never marketed . . . or is just plain silly.

How silly? So silly that the IRS has given the synfuels tax credit to companies that have done nothing but spray starch or diesel fuel or even Elmer's glue on coal.

Corporations, ranging from utilities to the Marriott hotel chain, have leapt through this loophole like wolves leaping for a lamb chop. The result is that they have dodged about $2 billion a year in taxes—a wad that the rest of us ordinary taxpayers have to make up, either in increased taxes or reduced services. This scam will soon grow to $10 billion a year, as more corporations have spied the lamb chop and are going for it.

Finally, the IRS decided to crack down by reviewing whether those companies' so-called synfuels actually worked. Yet even this long-overdue step was assailed by synfuel profiteers, their lobbyists, and their puppets in Congress, who went after the IRS, threatening the agency's enforcement budget and hauling the IRS commissioner to the woodshed. Unsurprisingly, the IRS recently succumbed to the corporate pressure.

A Dirty Dozen

Wheeze! Hack! Gasp! Gag! Bleeeeecch!

If America's air, water, global warming, and other enviro policies seem as if they're coming right out of a corporate smokestack, that's because they are.

Bush has not merely put our government in service to polluters and plunderers, he has put it directly into their hands. It's not just a matter of the corporate-hugging, cabinet-level sparklies at the top of Washington's environmental pyramid—Gale Norton (Interior), Mike Leavitt (EPA), Spencer Abraham (Energy), Ann Veneman (Ag). Rather, the daily dirty work is being done by dozens of industry no-names, trusted lobbyists, and ideological hacks whom Bush has installed in key positions deep inside the innards of the pyramid, where they are quietly but zealously reengineering the flow of national policy from pure public protection to poisonous private profits.

It's these subcabinet policy operatives that actually run government. Meet a Dirty Dozen of them:

1. **JAMES CONNAUGHTON,** chairman of the president's council on environmental quality. A former lobbyist for utilities, mining, chemical, and other industrial polluters, Connaughton represented the likes of General Electric and ARCO in their effort to escape responsibility for cleaning up toxic Superfund sites. Now he heads up pollution-policy development for the administration

and coordinates its implementation. He has led the charge to weaken the standards of getting arsenic out of our drinking water, and he has steadily advised Bush to ignore, divert, stall, dismiss, and otherwise block out all calls for action against the industrial causes of global warming.

2. **JOHN D. GRAHAM,** administrator of regulatory affairs in the White House budget office. Graham is the de facto boss of all regulatory programs for the entire government—any change in enviro rules must pass through his strangling hands. An avowed enemy of pollution regulations, he previously headed a quasi-academic front group that consistently issued reports claiming that environmental protections are too costly for industry—not a surprising stance since he and his "risk assessment" center were financed by more than a hundred corporate entities, including the American Petroleum Institute, Dow, DuPont, Exxon, Monsanto, and 3M.

3. **J. STEVEN GRILES,** deputy secretary of the Interior Department. A disciple of the infamous James Watt, for whom he worked in the Reagan years, Griles went on to be a lobbyist for the National Mining Association (NMA), Edison Electric, Chevron, Occidental Petroleum, and other energy giants. Appointed the overseer of America's 500 million acres of public lands, Griles was hailed by the NMA as "an ally of the industry," and the mining association welcomed him as "a breath of fresh air"—for polluters, of course, not for us air breathers! Even though he is a public official now, he still draws $284,000 a year from his former lobbying firm, which represents corporations he supposedly regulates. Also, he has continued to meet behind closed doors with his former (and perhaps future) industry clients. The inspector general is investigating him for the blatant conflicts of interest posed by these meetings, which he had pledged to avoid in a "recusal agreement" he signed to get his government job.

> **"** *Talk about a dream team. The oil industry may have found one in Interior Secretary Gale Norton and her newly nominated deputy, J. Steven Griles. . . . As expected, oil industry groups, looking to get more access to resource-rich federal lands, were gladdened by the nomination.* **"**
>
> —*Oil Daily*, **March 12, 2001**

4. **JEFFREY HOLMSTEAD,** assistant EPA administrator for air quality. Previously a lobbyist with the firm of Latham & Watkins, Holmstead represented electric utilities trying to fight air pollution restrictions, and he represented the Farm Bureau conglomerate in its fights against pesticide controls. Now inside, he's a key player pushing Bush's Clear Skies initiative, which will allow a 520 percent increase in toxic mercury pollution, a 225 percent jump in carbon dioxide pollution (a global warming contaminant), and a delay in the enforcement of smog and soot pollution until 2016. In charge of writing a new rule to limit mercury poisoning of children by electric power plants, Holmstead embraced a watered-down rule that essentially was written by his old lobbying firm of Latham & Watkins.

5. **WILLIAM HORN,** chairman of the fish and wildlife commission. In charge of charting policies governing America's priceless National Wildlife Refuge System, Horn's background is not that of a wildlife protector, but that of a corporate lobbyist representing interests wanting to exploit our public refuges for their profit. He has lobbied for Florida Power & Light, Yukon Pacific Corporation (which wants to build a gas pipeline from Alaska's North Slope to the port of Valdez, then export the gas to Asia), and the Nuclear Energy Institute. For a hint about his attitude toward preserving pristine wildlife areas, note that he has been the lead attorney for such outfits as the International Snowmobile Manufacturers Association, New Jersey Beach Buggy Association, and Sun Valley HeliSki company.

6. **WILLIAM G. MYERS III,** solicitor of the Interior Department. The government's top lawyer for cases involving exploitation of our public lands by mining and agribusiness corporations, Myers previously was a lawyer and lobbyist representing mining and agribusiness corporations. At Interior, he has pushed for new rules to allow more cattle grazing, to limit endangered species protections, to require fewer environmental impact statements for the lands under his stewardship, and to open public lands in five western states to oil drilling. Myers is under investigation by ethics officials for meeting with his former corporate clients despite having signed a conflict-of-interest agreement to avoid such contacts. Meanwhile, George W has nominated this possible law violator to be a federal appeals judge.

7. **BENNETT RALEY,** assistant interior secretary for water. A longtime extremist "corporate rights" advocate who previously lobbied to kill our nation's Clean Water Act, Raley now is the top official in charge of water issues at the Interior Department. In 2002, he teamed up with Karl Rove in a flagrant political maneuver to provide extra water for agribusiness from a federal water project in eastern Washington, even though agency scientists warned that this would be disastrous for wild salmon under federal protections in the Klamath River. Career agency professionals were forced to bow to White House political pressure, and thousands of fish died. When responsible officials tried to divert some of the Klamath basin water back to the endangered salmon populations, Raley again waved in Rove to apply top-heavy political pressure and back them off.

"Our goal is to destroy, to eradicate the environmental movement. We want to be able to exploit the environment for private gain."

—Ron Arnold, *founder of the corporate-funded Wise-Use movement that has placed many of its minions in key environmental positions in the Bush administration*

8. **MARK REY,** Agriculture Department undersecretary for natural resources. Rey, who now is caretaker of America's 156 national forests, has spent his entire career as a timber industry lobbyist and congressional staffer hell-bent on fattening industry profits by letting corporations clear-cut the public's trees. He headed the American Forest and Paper Association, the leading proponent of logging our national forests, prior to becoming a Senate staffer and authoring an infamous 1995 act that suspended all environmental laws to give the green light to corporations to clear-cut old-growth forests in the Pacific Northwest. He also wrote a bill that would have eliminated local citizen committees that oversee timber harvests. As forest chief, Rey has been the key force behind Bush's Healthy Forests scam that would allow nearly unlimited clear-cutting in pristine national forests.

9. **THOMAS SANSONETTI,** assistant attorney general for environment and natural resources. Now the public's lead lawyer for defending our environmental protection programs in court, Sansonetti is a Republican Party political operative and a lobbyist from Wyoming who represented coal companies and other energy corporations in their efforts to undermine these same environmental protections. He previously was chief lawyer for the Republican National Committee. As a lobbyist, he pushed in Washington to let each coal company increase its mining on federal lands by one third. Another of the far-right corporatists that Bush has put in charge of the machinery of government, Sansonetti is a proud member of the government-hating laissez-faire Federalist Society, which is amply funded by ultraconservative corporate foundations.

10. **PATRICIA LYNN SCARLETT,** assistant interior secretary for policy. This overseer of overall policy affecting our nation's public resources is no fan of the public even holding resources, and doesn't like regulation of private efforts to exploit the public's re-

sources. She has written that "environmentalism is a coherent philosophy that rivals Marxism." Most of Scarlett's career has been spent with the Reason Foundation, a think tank that vigorously opposes government regulations and is funded by such corporations as Chevron, Dow, Enron, ExxonMobil, Philip Morris, and Shell Oil, as well as by the American Petroleum Institute, American Plastics Council, and American Chemistry Council.

11. **CARMEN TOOHEY,** special interior assistant for Alaska. Cam, as she is known, is Gale Norton's handpicked aide to oversee environmental policies affecting the vast federal landholdings in our nation's largest state. For the Bushites, policy priority number one in Alaska is, of course, to turn loose their oil buddies to build roads, move in drilling rigs, and extend pipelines across the majestic Arctic National Wildlife Refuge. Cam is well versed on this priority and completely in tune with it, for she comes to her government job from having led Arctic Power, a lobbying group supporting corporate interests that want to open our public refuge to their private profit schemes.

12. **REBECCA WATSON,** assistant interior secretary for land and minerals. Directing the Bureau of Land Management, Watson is responsible for the rules and fees for gold-mining companies, drillers, and other corporations wanting to profit on the wealth of minerals and other public resources within our federal lands. Her qualifications for the job are not as a public defender, but as a Montana lawyer representing mining and logging corporations that either wanted unfettered access to these public treasures or didn't want to pay for the environmental damage done by their exploitative procedures. Watson has represented Golden Sunlight Mines, Fidelity Exploration, Plum Creek Timber, and other companies regulated by the agency she now heads. She also worked on the litigation committee of the right-wing Mountain States Legal Foundation, a litigious, corporate-funded group of legal activists

that tries to run over any environmental protection that pinches even a dime's worth of ill-gotten corporate profits.

Inside the "Pink Zone"

I have seen the future, and it is this: gas masks.

As Bush & Company dismantle America's health, safety, and environmental protections at the behest of such mass polluters as the oil, chemical, coal, nuclear, and auto industries, some critics have rudely accused them of selling out the public's health and safety just to satisfy Bush's campaign contributors. I disagree. George himself has told us that he's a compassionate conservative, and while his conservative side says industry must be free to contaminate us, I believe his compassionate side also has a plan, which is to issue gas masks to everyone.

Indeed, this is what his Federal Emergency Management Agency (FEMA) is doing in Anniston, Alabama. During the next several years, the army will incinerate some 660,000 of the chemical weapons stored at its Anniston Depot—deadly stuff like sarin, mustard gas, and an extra-lethal chemical called "VX agent." Understandably, the good people of Anniston are less than thrilled, since their homes, schools, hospitals, day-care centers, and whatnot are in an area that the army delicately labels the "pink zone."

Not to worry, though, for the local citizenry is the first community in America to receive government-issued gas masks from the Bush administration. Seven million dollars have been allocated by FEMA to provide protective gas hoods and suits for 35,000 people. Poking through the kit she was given, Brenda Lindell said: "You think that's going to keep me safe? I don't think so!"

I wonder: Do you keep this gear in your home? In your car? Your briefcase? Do kids carry it to school in their backpacks? A killer gas plume can cover the whole area in eight minutes. What if you're in the shower or have the radio on when the alarm goes off announc-

OOPS

Only six months after the Anniston incinerator began operating, an "incident" happened at the supposedly foolproof facility. Alarms sounded, terrifying locals, but officials rushed out to say it was only a minute leak of sarin. But minute can be massive—just a drop of sarin can kill. On-edge residents noted that they were told such incidents, no matter how tiny, would not occur. If it's so safe, what say we base Donnie Rumsfeld and his family there until the burning is complete?

ing an accident? "Even a small accident could be catastrophic," says the county emergency director. Then there's the fact that while the feds will issue 35,000 masks, 75,000 people live within nine miles of the incinerator. I guess compassion can only stretch so far.

Local resident Rufus Kinney spoke for me when he said: "*This is absolute madness.*" He added that "The irony is that our government is looking for weapons of mass destruction in Iraq, and at the same time, they're not protecting us from our own weapons of mass destruction."

Messing with Frogs

As you can see on TV's various nature shows, it's often a brutal world out there, with one critter devouring another. But at least that's the natural cycle, and I find it a whole lot less fearsome than this recent *New York Times* (April 17, 2002) headline: "Weed Killer Deforms Sex Organs in Frogs."

Hello! We're not talking about a single critter being devoured as some other critter's dinner, but about the reproductive capability of a *whole species* of critter being messed with in the most unnatural ways. The National Academy of Science reported that young male frogs living in water containing very low doses of the weed killer atrazine develop multiple sex organs or develop both male and female sex organs.

Atrazine is the most commonly used weed killer in the United States, widely sprayed on our lawns, fields, roadsides, golf courses . . . all over. This toxic chemical, however, doesn't just kill weeds and go away. With such poisons, there is no "away." Atrazine residue runs off into our waterways, and it's now found in our drinking water, groundwater, streams, snow runoff, etc.—even rain contains atrazine. As the lead scientist of the frog study said: "There is virtually no atrazine-free environment."

You could ask the frogs what that means. Atrazine causes male frog cells to produce an enzyme that converts their testosterone to estrogen, perverting their sexuality and destroying their reproductivity. This is happening at a much lower level of atrazine contamination than was previously considered to be a problem. Indeed, the Environmental Protection Agency allows three parts per billion (ppb) of atrazine in our drinking water. Yet the frog mutation is taking place in water with only one tenth of one part per billion of contamination.

Are we at risk? "I'm not saying it's safe for humans," the research leader said. "I'm not saying it's unsafe for humans. All I'm saying is that it makes hermaphrodites of frogs."

Dumping High-Tech Toxins on Poor Nations

Alas, it's not only the old, dirty industries soiling our planet. Bill Gates, Michael Dell, and the other pooh-bahs of high-techery not only like to gloat about their computer wizardry and business success, they also brag that theirs is a "clean industry" and that they are corporate environmentalists.

They might try selling that load of crap to the people around Guiya, China. This is one of the low-wage hellholes that America's high-tech executives use as a dumping ground for their electronics waste, which includes some 45 million computers that are discarded annually. The dirty little secret of the industry is that their computers are loaded with toxins, and a report called "Exporting Harm: The Techno-Trashing of Asia" (produced by a group of five environmental organizations) reveals that these poisons are causing environmental and health disasters in the lands where they're dumped, far from the sight and out of the minds of the billionaires who profit from selling them.

Technically, says the industry, the discarded electronics are not dumped; they're "recycled." In reality, what happens is that poor Asians are paid a pittance to scavenge various metals and other re-salable compounds out of these machines. Indeed, about 100,000 people, including thousands of children, in Guiya toil in the midst of piles of electronic trash, using acid to extract traces of gold, dumping cathode-ray tubes filled with lead, opening toner cartridges by hand to brush the toxic toner into buckets, and burning plastic components. Guiya's groundwater is now so polluted that the people have to truck in water for human use.

> **"Whipping may be imposed to punish toxic waste polluters."**
>
> —*A 1996 enforcement rule adopted in Malaysia*

While Europe is moving to require its computer makers to accept disposal responsibility for their hazardous products, industry lobbyists here have stifled any such moves. Also, while there's a 1989 international treaty to limit the export of toxic wastes, the United States is the only developed country that has refused to sign it.

Democrats Get Down and Dirty, Too

Some days I don't know whether to laugh, cry, or go bowling.

On the one hand, I'm pleased that Democrats in Congress have been doing a proper job of lambasting George W and his gang of congressional whores who've shown an insatiable lust for delivering special legislative favors to any corporate lobbyist waving a campaign check. Yet just when you start to cheer for these Democrats, their leader gets caught slinking down the same trashy back streets that the Republicans work. In 2001, on the night of December 20, just hours before Congress adjourned for the year, there was Democratic Senate leader Tom Daschle slipping a little ol' provision into the "miscellaneous" section of the Pentagon's appropriation bill.

Tom's amendment had been written by Patton Boggs, a powerhouse Washington lobbying firm, on behalf of Barrick Gold—a Canadian outfit that's one of the biggest mining corporations in the world. It seems that Barrick owns a massive gold mine in Tom's state of South Dakota. This multibillion-dollar mine has now played out, and Barrick wants to close it. However, gold mining is an environmentally brutish and toxic process, so this mine is in line to become another Superfund site, potentially costing the company $40 million to clean up.

Guess what Daschle's little ol' amendment does? It exempts Barrick Gold from "any and all liability relating to the mine"! It exonerates this corporation for all "damages to natural resources or the environment." Moreover, if anyone sues Barrick for the mess it left, Daschle obligates Uncle Sam to defend the Canadian corporation in court and reimburse it for any losses. Also, Tom's amendment waives the sovereign immunity of the U.S. government, allowing the Canadian firm to sue us if they're not happy. Meanwhile, all costs of the cleanup are shifted to you and me, the sadsack taxpayers.

Who needs enemies like Republicans when we've got "friends" like Tom going whoring, too?

Timber Scams

Time for another Hightower "Hog Report."

Check out these oinkers. There are giant timber and paper companies that are granted logging privileges in America's national forests. They're granted much more than the privilege to log, however. We taxpayers also provide millions of dollars in annual subsidies by letting the corporations take our trees at waaaay below the market price; plus, we even build thousands of miles of logging roads in the forests to make it easier and cheaper for them to take the timber out.

Mother Jones magazine has reported that the U.S. Forest Service is now doing them an extra-special favor by providing an additional high-tech *cosmetic* subsidy. It amounts to a corporate PR scam, paid for by you and me. It's a $3 million state-of-the-art computer software program that helps the loggers hide their environment-destroying, clear-cutting practices from the public eye. Basically, it's a computerized game of hide-and-seek. To reduce the public's outrage at coming to a national forest and seeing acres and acres of stumps where majestic thousand-year-old trees once stood, computer programs with names like "Smart Forest" and "Virtual Forest" allow the corporations to analyze the terrain so their clear-cuts can be done behind ridges, down in ravines, and on the back side of mountains. These out-of-sight, out-of-mind software programs are being put in all eight hundred forest service offices.

The forest service also helps the companies create "beauty strips" along the tourist roads—a veneer of trees that look great as you drive along, but behind the strip and beyond your view is the distressing sight of our magnificent forests entirely stripped of their trees. All of this is the forest service's way of letting us "have" our forests, while letting the timber hogs eat them.

Kill Endangered Species to Save Them

I thought I was beyond astonishment. I've been to the state fair twice, I've participated in Texas politics, and I've dug into the thievery of Wall Street and Washington . . . but I've never seen such mind-numbing stupidity as this proposal from George W's Interior Department.

The boneheads in charge of administering our nation's policies toward the world's endangered species have decided that the way to "save" Asian elephants, Amazon parrots, and other species threatened with extinction . . . is to kill them!

What we have here is more of the ivory tower, laissez-faire bushwa that substitutes for thinking in this corporatized administration. Their assertion is that if America's pet industry, circus companies, fur and skin purveyors, and safari firms were able to, ahem, "harvest" a big bunch of these already endangered animals each year, these corporations would pay harvest fees for each animal taken, thus allowing governments in these impoverished countries to funnel the money into better conservation programs for the animals that survive.

It would be akin to letting a crime syndicate pay fees for its own heists so local police could fund crime prevention lectures.

Of course, in the real world, what this harebrained scheme would do is put a price on the head of every animal, providing an irresistible and uncontrollable market incentive for freelance entrepreneurs to kill, ship, and profit from endangered wildlife.

Yet Interior Department officials are pushing blindly and unilaterally ahead with their executive "reinterpretation" of the Endangered Species Act, simply dismissing anyone who protests. As one Bushite scoffed: "There are critics who are going to claim some kind of ulterior motive" to our action.

Yes, *me!* The motive is your mindless determination to twist all laws to serve your perverse corporate ideology.

BIRDBRAINED

Out in the Pacific Ocean is a small island that the U.S. Navy wanted to use for target practice. While no humans live there, it provides essential habitat for various birds that are protected by the Migratory Bird Treaty.

Navy lawyers argued before a federal judge in 2002 that, although the shelling of the island would certainly kill the bulk of the birds, it would not totally eliminate the species, and this could be a better result than killing no birds at all:

"*In some respects bird watchers get more enjoyment spotting a rare bird than they do spotting a common one.*"

The judge sided with the birds.

Putting the "Yuck" in Yucca Mountain

I know what we should do with the high-level atomic waste generated by our country's nuclear power plants—let's put it in the hole in Spencer Abraham's head.

Spencer is the former senator from Michigan who, in his one term in office, distinguished himself by being the top recipient of energy industry money, including an arsenal of cash from the nuke power boys. He was quickly dismissed by Michigan voters, but George W and his nuclear power backers rescued Abraham from well-deserved obscurity by ensconcing him as secretary of energy. Now, when energy lobbyists shout "Jump, froggie!" Abraham dutifully asks, "How high?"

So far Secretary Abraham has rubber-stamped the long-held desire of nuclear utility lobbyists to ship all of the industry's current and future atomic wastes to Yucca Mountain, just ninety miles from Las Vegas. The industry wants us taxpayers to bury all of its waste inside this desert mountain, thus freeing the utilities from responsibility for cleaning up their own radioactive messes and letting them make even more nuclear waste.

Problem is, Yucca Mountain is smack-dab in the middle of one of the most active earthquake zones in the country, with thirty-three known geological faults crisscrossing the area, fracturing the rock, and creating pathways for the radiation to flow into the area's drinking water. In the past twenty-five years, more than six hundred sizable earthquakes have hit this area, including a magnitude 5.6 earthquake that did a million dollars in damage to one of the Department of Energy's own field offices, set up to study whether it was safe to bury this stuff in Yucca Mountain.

But even an earthquake can't crack though Spencer's thick skull, so he has done exactly what the lobbyists put him there to do: He has formally recommended that Yucca Mountain be America's nuclear waste dump.

What a deal! Nuclear power corporations get billions of dollars in subsidies from us taxpayers, then they get all the profits from the energy that is sold, and in exchange they want to give us taxpayers their nuclear waste—all 77,000 tons of it. Not only is this another multibillion-dollar giveaway to these private profit-making corporations, but it's a deadly move for the rest of us. It would require convoys of trucks and railcars to haul their waste, cutting a new radioactive trail across forty-two states and through dozens of cities.

George W, who is loaded with campaign cash from the nuke boys and is eager to please them, has okayed their scheme. It's safe, he declared. Sure, George, about as safe as letting the baby play with a hand grenade. In fact, Bush is so eager to do this corporate favor that he okayed the scheme *before* the Energy Department even designed the canisters that are supposed to hold this hot waste for ten thousand years, *before* it knows how to seal the tunnels that will hold the canisters, *before* it solved the rather large problem of water corroding the canisters, and *before* some three hundred other scientific and engineering questions have been resolved.

Bush & Company claims that these are mere technical matters that someone can deal with later, even though independent scientific experts scoff at this idea. Unfortunately, the Bushites' cluelessness is explosive.

Guess Who Loves Conservation?

When it comes to meeting our nation's energy needs, Dick Cheney and George W are power hawks. Let's drill and build, they holler! No sissified conservation programs for them—they're after oil, gas, coal, and nukes.

But wait a minute, guess whose official residence uses geothermal heat pumps and has been thoroughly retrofitted to conserve energy, making it a model for the new-age thinking he so volubly scorns? Dick Cheney's! And guess who was so impressed by the money-saving energy efficiency of heat pumps that he installed one in his new house on the ranchette he bought in Texas? George W!

If it works for them, why not for the country? Money, honey. The Big Energy boys pumped millions into the Bush-Cheney election, and in return, they were allowed to write the energy policy that Dick and George are now pushing. So, while Bush and

FACTOID

When the Bush-Cheney energy plan was published, not only were solar, wind, and other renewable energy sources stiffed, but the Energy Department robbed $135,615 from the meager budget of the renewables program to pay for printing the report.

Cheney personally benefit from conservation, they ridicule it publicly, saying it might be a "personal virtue," but "not a sufficient basis for a sound, comprehensive energy policy."

But wait another minute. Guess who has found out that conservation actually is a very sound basis for energy policy? Electric utilities! From the Washington, D.C., area out to Seattle, utilities all across the country have invested billions in conservation programs, ranging from retrofitting homes to offering rebates to customers who use less electricity.

These programs work, they're cheaper than building new power plants, they're nonpolluting . . . and customers love them. A manager at Sacramento, California's municipal utility, which offers twenty different conservation programs for consumers, told the *New York Times,* "Our phones are just ringing off the hook." Thanks to conservation, Sacramento avoided California's rolling blackouts of 2001 as well as the costs of building a huge new power plant.

The Bush-Cheney energy policy ought to be based on what's in their own homes, not what's in their campaign fund.

Energetic Thieves

Whenever you hear that Washington is moving forward with "comprehensive" legislation to do this or that, it means that some larger-than-usual theft is under way.

Beware, then, of the "comprehensive energy bill" that the White House is now trying to—choo-choo cha-boogie!—railroad through the legislative system. This boondoggle even comes wrapped in the flag, as the Bushites try to capitalize on their military victory over Saddam by claiming that America's "energy independence" is dependent on this glob of special-interest gimmies.

Buried in it are $18.7 billion in tax subsidies for ExxonMobil, BP, Shell, and the other global oil and gas giants and for the electric utility greedheads that keep raising our rates as they pollute our air. The congressional sponsors use Orwellian terms to make it seem as though they are working in the public interest by taking actions that "streamline," bring "balance," provide "relief," allow "flexibility," and otherwise do good things, when in fact they're just engaged in the same old special-interest gotcha.

For example:

- Their bill would allow oil corporations to escape paying the taxes they owe to We the People on the gas they take out of the Gulf of Mexico.
- It would let the federal government overrule states that dare to tell utilities they can't run electric power lines over your land or through your community.
- It would make it harder for local citizens, farmers, environmentalists, and others to stop utilities that want to flood your area with hydroelectric dams.
- It would cut the royalties that these energy giants pay to us taxpayers to take the oil and gas from our public lands.
- It would let coal companies escape paying the health benefits of mine workers who've worked hard all their lives and come up with lungs full of killer coal dust.
- And the bill would open all of America's coastal water to oil and gas drilling.

Shifting the Cleanup Burden

Did your mother ever tell you that if you made a mess it was yours to clean up?

This is basic stuff. Taught by parents to children probably throughout the world, this admonition is part of America's cultural core, central to our ethical belief that we must be responsible for what we do. Even very young children understand this lesson in

THE PATH TO PROGRESS

Even if Bush, Congress, and a coterie of corporatist judges were not whacking at our antipollution protections like some crazed crew of plaid-clad Paul Bunyans on crack cocaine, we'd still be falling behind.

The Research Council of the National Academies, a twenty-five-member panel of our country's top scientific experts (more prestigious than that you cannot get), reported in January that even America's pre-Bush environmental laws were inadequate to prevent industry's various exhaust pipes from gagging us, undermining human health, and further poisoning our planet. While our country's environmental cleanup laws have been very successful per unit (of car, smokestack, etc.), they can't keep up with the ever-expanding growth in units.

So the science crowd says that, far from loosening pollution restrictions as we're now doing, we have to tighten them just to stay even . . . and then tighten them even more if we're to get ahead of the contaminants.

life, but there are some grown-ups who seem completely unable to grasp the concept. For example, industrial polluters are among the poutiest, most willful violators of this childhood rule.

Toxic polluters prefer to make the mess, grab the profits, and run. That's why the Superfund waste cleanup law was passed in 1980. "The polluter pays" was the rallying cry, and the law was needed because polluters engaged in so many shell games to avoid their cleanup responsibilities. This law assessed a tax on corporations that contaminate our air, water, and communities, with the money going into a trust fund that pays for cleanups at especially nasty industrial sites.

Of course, industry executives threw little tantrums about being taxed, but the Superfund law has worked to clean up about five hundred of their messes. In 1995, however, Congress finally caved in to the industry's whining and eliminated the tax, which had amassed a fund of nearly $4 billion. By 2001, however, the fund had dropped to $28 million. Yet there were still huge "megasites" to clean up, costing more than $200 million each—plus, industry is still out there, creating more Superfund messes all the time.

So here comes George W to the rescue . . . of the polluters! Despite the obvious need, he rejected restoration of the corporate tax to bolster the Superfund. He says the polluter tax is "burdensome" to industry, so instead of making polluters pay, he'll simply clean up fewer places . . . and shift all the cleanup cost to us taxpayers.

If George thinks the tax is "burdensome," he ought to try being among the polluted who live next to industry's Super-messes.

The Grassroots Water Rebellion

Where's the department of Homeland Security when we really need it?

I suppose homeland czar Tom Ridge is too busy with his ever-changing palette of color codes to notice or care that dozens of American communities presently find themselves under assault by

NAME THAT ENVIRO!

You think "greenies" are kooky today? How about the well-known fellow of nearly a century ago who put up bat houses around his yard to control mosquitoes organically, who relished serving lunches of "grass sandwiches," who was a passionate bird-watcher and conservationist, and who dressed in suits made of soybean fabric! Who was this flake? Answer on next page.

foreign powers with names like Suez Lyonnaise, Vivendi, and Per-rier. These global corporate raiders are grabbing for our most es-sential public resource: water.

While politicians—from Congress to city halls—have been bamboozled by privatization hucksters who promise to bring "market efficiency" to the distribution of scarce water, ordinary folks have shown themselves to be way warier of surrendering pub-lic control. They know instinctively that the corporations are sim-ply trying to grab a monopoly over a substance no one can live without, then squeeze maximum profits from it.

The great story here, untold by the establishment media, is of courageous rebels who are daring to step in front of the Great Cor-porate Water Rush. Meet one. Hiroshi Kanno, sixty-four, works a small farm in central Wisconsin. He stands only five feet six inches tall, but with his family and neighbors, he became a giant killer, beginning in 2000, when the multibillion-dollar Perrier Group ar-rived in the towns of Newport, Rhode Island, and New Haven, Connecticut. Perrier informed startled locals that it had a won-drous plan to begin continuous pumping of five hundred gallons per minute of the area's pure spring water into its assorted bottles (Perrier's labels include Arrowhead, Calistoga, Deer Park, Oasis, Ozarka, Poland Springs, and Utopia). It seemed a done deal, be-cause Perrier had the backing of then-governor Tommy Thompson (now the secretary of health), whose natural resources agency quickly obliged Perrier with pumping permits.

Henry Ford! He practiced green in his business, too. In 1933, two bushels of soybeans went into every Ford car—the paint, body, horn button, accelerator pedal, door handles, and timing gears were made of materials derived from soybeans.

But Kanno asked, "Who needs this?" He and others began asking more pointed questions, but got only evasive answers, so they got to organizing, with "Perrier Go Away" as their rallying cry. With the help of Ed Garvey, the savvy and scrappy people's lawyer from Madison, Wisconsin, they sued the state to revoke the permits and also launched referendums in both Newport and New Haven.

Perrier responded with hired lobbyists, a PR offensive, and cash—including giving $20,000 to the city of New Haven. But money didn't buy love. New Haven voted three to one against the water scheme, and Newport voted four to one against it. New Haven went further, voting overwhelmingly to recall the town chairman who had accepted Perrier's $20,000; then they gave the money back. "This is about the people versus the powers that be," said the new town manager. Perrier still retains local water leases, but Kanno and his group forced it to leave their towns, and a state judge has now ruled that the state erred in granting the permits.

Polluting the Poor

Woody Allen said, "Money is better than poverty, if only for financial reasons."

And for health reasons, too, Woody.

That's because things like toxic waste dumps and chemical plants seem to have a special affinity for poor neighborhoods . . . along with a remarkable aversion to the enclaves of the wealthy.

Pollution is a bully, you see, and it always pursues the path of least resistance, which has led straight into low-income communities, especially minority neighborhoods.

If you live in a poor neighborhood, chances are good that you're next door to some undesirables: a lead smelter, a toxic incinerator, a gasoline storage tank.

And if you live in a minority, low-income neighborhood, your chances of environmental unpleasantness roughly doubles. In fact,

60 percent of black and Latino Americans live in communities with at least one toxic-waste site. This means their neighbors are people like Ms. Benzene, Mr. Lead, the Dioxins, Monsieur Toluene, and other chemicals that cause everything from constant headaches to cancer.

And to think I was mad about that barking dog next door.

To add insult to injury, it turns out that our government regulators are much more lenient on corporations that pollute in communities of color. The average fine for hazardous-waste pollution in a white neighborhood is $333,000. In a minority community? $55,000.

But these folks are not just getting fed up, they're acting up. Black residents in Chicago forced the owner of an abandoned paint factory to come back and clean up his mess. Mexican-Americans in California's San Joaquin Valley blocked construction of a toxic-waste incinerator. Wallace, Louisiana, took on the Formosa Plastics Corporation and scuttled its plans to build a wood pulp and rayon factory.

Then there's Convent, Louisiana.

Here's the score there: People 1, Shintech 0.

Citizens of this small town scored big against Shintech, a giant Japanese chemical corporation. Convent, a town with a mostly low-income black population, had been locked in a struggle for months with Shintech, which planned to build a plant making more than a billion pounds of PVC—polyvinyl chloride—a year.

The people considered this a textbook case of environmental injustice—another big polluter coming in and feeling free to dump on them because their town presumably was too poor and too powerless to fight back. Indeed, corporate executives admitted that their plans included the release of some 600,000 pounds of toxic air contaminants a year from this factory. That's an annual diet of about 300 pounds of toxics (many known to be cancer-causers) for every man, woman, and child in Convent.

To the surprise of Shintech and the Louisiana political establishment, though, the people rebelled, saying they already lived in a "cancer alley" of petrochemical plants and were not going to take it anymore. Organized as Citizens for Jobs and the Environment, they got noisy, got some legal help, and got to agitating. It was a David-and-Goliath battle, with the folks of Convent fighting not only that corporation but also their own governor at the time, Mike Foster, who'd been thoroughly polluted with petrochemical campaign contributions.

But it's the governor who gagged. The people applied such political and media heat that Shintech had to announce it would withdraw from Convent. "Hallelujah and praise the Lord," cried Mary Louise Green, one of the folks who'd been fighting the plant. "Honey, do you know how long I've been praying for that?" she exclaimed.

Prayers are good, but so is agitating and organizing. As the people of Convent showed, the Lord helps those who help themselves.

> **" *Three things—and three things only—sustain life on this planet. They are: a thin layer of soil, a cover of atmosphere, and a little rainfall. That is all the Lord has given us. Except one thing: He has given us a choice of what we do with it. We can waste it. We can pollute it. We can neglect it. Or we can conserve it, and we can protect it, and we can develop it, and we can pass it on to our children more promising, more abundant than we received it. "***
> —*Lyndon B. Johnson, September 25, 1964*

BUSHWORD PUZZLE

ACROSS

1. Punishment Malaysia imposes on toxic-waste polluters
7. Former president who looks like the Jolly Green Giant compared to George W
8. Appropriate emotional response to George W's enviro policies
9. What causes more pollution than automobiles, according to Ronald Reagan
10. Appropriate shape for mountaintops, according to coal industry
12. What Rush Limbaugh calls the ozone hole
13. Mountain dumping place for atomic waste, 90 miles from Las Vegas
15. Per LBJ, one of the three ingredients necessary for life on Earth
17. Men's undergarments, or what George W calls reading
18. Ingredient Henry Ford used in making his suits and cars

DOWN

2. Heroic early settler or someone who buys favors from the Bush administration
3. Bush solution for global warming: "Get an_____"
4. _____ Forest: name of software U.S. Forest Service uses to hide logger clear-cutting in national forests
5. What one feels as so many environmental protections are eliminated
6. Word Bushites chanted to make carbon dioxide magically disappear as a pollutant
9. Secret ingredient inside your Dell computer
11. What we will all be without the ozone layer
14. Winged creatures that keep getting in the way of navy bombing
16. Polluters are running _____ in Washington

Solution on page 225.

Cheap Underwear, Bub

☞ *By subsidizing CEOs who move our jobs offshore, George is saving you and me a dime on every pair of made-in-China shorts we buy.*

"*Oh* beautiful, for spacious malls . . ." Is this a great country, or what?

Thanks to our leaders' unblinking faith in the theory of free-market globalism, our country is being freed from having to make anything! America no longer has to produce food, we're fast moving beyond the need for those messy blue-collar manufacturing plants, and now, quicker than you can say Islamabad, we won't have to do our own high-tech work either. With another four years of Bush, America will reach that long-sought utopian ideal of a nation based on 100 percent pure consumerism.

Forget that old image of "hog butcher for the world" or even computer programmers of the world, shopping is us! It's now what we do, who we are, defining us in this marvelous American

Millennium as the greatest superpower ever. (OK, our military also helps with this definition, but don't forget that the Pentagon is by far the most voracious shop-till-you-drop consumer ever invented, so it still comes back to our proud national ethic of acquisition.)

Some of us go to Neiman Marcus, some to Wal-Mart, but we all have our roles to play in this fabulous, phantasmagoric consumer economy of ours. That's why you need a president who's dedicated to keeping global wages low and corporate profits high, for that's what keeps your shelves stocked to the roof with ever more of those baubles, bangles, beads, and shiny bling-bling we love to buy from the Republic of Whogivesadamn. It's the economy, stupid.

Oh, I can hear you liberal carpers weeping and moaning about jobs for the "American middle class." Give me a bleeping break, Marx-breath. What's so great about being middle class? Who wants to program software or make cars just so you can fit somewhere in the middle of economic achievement? Any country can provide the engineers and be the makers of stuff—let all those teeming hordes of impoverished little people in Mexico and India do that. Better to be on the receiving end of the stuff. It's about rising above the muddling middle, my friends.

Luckily, we've got the Man with the Plan already in the White House, a man who's leading us Americans to our rightful destiny as a nation of upscale consumers. Even after the terrorist attacks of September 11, he did not lose his steady vision, did he? Certainly not. Instead, he bravely rallied us as a nation to (and I still get goose bumps just thinking about the majesty of his words) "Go shopping." Now that's leadership.

And don't give me that crybaby left-wing socialistic jabberwocky about people left behind. Yes, I realize that there are some who are shopping-impaired, who just don't have what it takes to be upscale, but our national leaders have the moral responsibility to focus on those of us who make our country strong through our muscular consumerism rather than on the consumer weaklings. Need I remind you that George W. Bush has already met this test of moral leadership with his three (count them, three!) tax cuts for the rich in three years? And don't forget that these cuts include a special $100,000 deduction for businesses that buy Hummers for their top executives! See, this is a guy with his eye squarely on the prize.

Besides, there will still be plenty of jobs for the drones—we'll always need more prison guards, for example, and there's no shortage of work for people who can handle a leafblower or are willing to wear a hairnet.

Let that Democrat bunch whine about the loss of middle-class opportunity. Give me a president who believes in his heart that anyone can be rich . . . if only they deserve it.

GEORGE W DOES THE ECONOMY

Carly Fiorina is a Bushite kind of woman: Donnie Rumsfeld with nail polish, a female with Dick Cheney belligerence and Darwinian ethics—let the strongest survive. Everyone else: adios, suckers.

Fiorina is honcha of the high-tech conglomerate Hewlett-Packard, and she is among the current spate of CEO enthusiasts for offshoring any and all U.S. jobs, especially the well-paying middle-class jobs that her corporation once was proud to provide. Hey, the notion that corporations supposedly have social responsibilities is so last century. This is the 2004 Carly-eat-dog world of global gotcha. *"There is no job that is America's God-given right anymore,"* she bellowed last year, just before she announced more offshoring and bit off the head of a screeching American eagle. **[Publisher's Correction:** Sorry. The author mistakenly transposed the subjects in the aforementioned anecdote. It was not Ms. Fiorina but Dick Cheney who bit off the eagle's head. The author regrets the error and apologizes if anyone was offended or is at all squeamish about seeing corporate policy in action.]

Carly Fiorina is proof that the X chromosome is every bit as capable as the Y when it comes to producing skinflinted, cold-blooded CEOs who never met a worker they wouldn't trade for a few pennies less in wages, even if that means abandoning America itself and moving all jobs to Pakistan, Kakistan, or Lower Helland-backistan.

And, in George W, Carly and her CEO cohorts have found their champion. By February of this year, Bush had provided so many governmental goodies for them that the rest of us were taking notice of his corporate servitude. Polls ranked Bush's handling of the economy lower than the public's approval of pedophile priests, so the White House finally responded with bold and decisive action: They convened a conference. Dubbed an Economic

> **"So the question is, do corporate executives, provided they stay within the law, have responsibilities in their business activities other than to make as much money for their shareholders as possible? And my answer to that is, no they do not."**
>
> *—Milton Friedman,*
> *economist and patron saint of Bushanomics*

Roundtable, participants who huddled with the president included the broad spectrum of Americans who are concerned about our economy—their diversity ranged all the way from the CEO of General Motors to the CEO of Goldman Sachs. No representatives of working people; no small farmers or Main Street business owners; no credit-card debtors, retirees, or single moms; no unemployed high school grads or out-of-luck Ph.D.'s—no Joe or Jolene Hardrow had a seat at Bush's table.

Well, said White House mouthpiece Scott McClellan, this was not a meeting for riffraff, but a classy gathering of "economic leaders," an "opportunity for the president to highlight his six-point plan for strengthening the economy *even more.*"

Even more?

- *Even more* than the 2.2 million jobs lost, disappeared, extinguished, poofed in just three years of Bush's term—the worst job performance since Herbert Hoover?

- *Even more* than the slowest wage growth in forty years with weekly pay stubs for middle- and low-income workers now falling behind inflation—which is to say the American majority is losing ground?

- *Even more* than today's crushing level of consumer debt, with families now shelling out 13 percent of their household income just to make interest payments to bankers—a level never seen

"Jobs are on the rise."
—George W, January 2004

Shortly after this pronouncement, the Labor Department reported that, indeed, 1,000 jobs had been created in the entire U.S. in the previous month. Meanwhile, on Bush's presidential watch, a total of 2.2 million jobs had been *lost.*

YOU DO THE MATH!

Based on the December rate of 1,000 jobs a month being created, how many years would it take just to replace the 2.2 million jobs lost in the Bush economy?

since the feds began keeping these records (and by the way, a level of interest far higher than what prompted Jesus to throw the moneychangers out of the temples)?

- *Even more* than the 1.6 million families (90 percent of them middle class) forced to file for bankruptcy this year—more than will suffer a heart attack, more than will graduate from college—not to mention the 9 million more families already in credit counseling, or the many millions more just one layoff from bankruptcy?

- *Even more* than having already added 1.4 million people to the poverty rolls, 2 million more to the list of Americans without health coverage, and millions more who've had their pension payments slashed or eliminated?

Please, Scott, don't y'all do anything more for us, you hear?

✳ **Sparklie Sighting** ✳ Maybe you weren't at the Economic Roundtable to hobnob with George, Michael Dell, and all the other offshoring swells, but one who did get the golden invite was our gal Carly! Yes, and after the confab, she stepped before the glom of media, as a beaming White House staff looked on, and gave witness that all of the corporate leaders who attended were (and this is a direct quote) "quite enthusiastic" about George's economic program.

Of course! Why wouldn't they be? Let's count some specific reasons for their giddiness, focusing just on the single category of government assistance that the Bushites provide specifically to facilitate corporate wanderlust: (1) *direct subsidies* to finance the moving of corporate operations to low-wage nations and to insure them against risk; (2) a whole new 2004 *package of corporate tax breaks* for moving offshore, including one for constructing factories in foreign nations; (3) *privatization* of 425,000 government jobs, specifically allowing the corporate contractors to move these tax-paid jobs out of our country; (4) nonstop negotiation of more *NAFTAesque trade scams* that grease the skids for CEOs wanting to produce their goods abroad, then sell them back here in the good ol' USA; (5) taxpayer-financed *trade junkets* that open the doors of foreign officialdom to corporate executives eager to relocate their factories, call centers, professional services, and other work outside the United States; and (6) sponsorship of *offshoring workshops,* held in such luxurious locations as New York City's Waldorf-Astoria hotel, to teach companies how to move their operations to China.

What's going on here is not merely the wholesale movement of our best jobs, but the deconstruction of America's middle class. With the full support of Bush (and, sad to say, of too many congressional Democrats), Carly and other top dogs have made a conscious choice to cut the leash, to sever the good fortune of America's corporate investor elites from any responsibility, affinity, or identity with the well-being of the mass of people with whom they supposedly share a country.

They are free, of course, to choose to separate their corporate and personal selves from us, but We the People have choices, too.

We can and should decide to separate the larger public interest from their self-interest. Let's take back the special tax breaks, enormous subsidies, regulatory advantages, political privileges, and all the other public favors that we have bestowed upon them. In every case, they've gotten these favors on the grounds that all of us would benefit from the advantages they were given. This trickle-down rationale was never true, but now they're even abandoning any pretense that they owe anything back.

Since they're unilaterally asserting that they have no obligation to us, we have no obligation to them. They're the ones wanting to take the *pluribus* out of *e pluribus unum,* so let's send the *unums* off on their own, without the financial backing of us *pluribus.*

A Work in Progress

Where'd we get this thing called the middle class?

It just comes with the territory, doesn't it? We're led to believe that it's a national birthright bestowed by the creation of America itself, extending from sea to shining sea, assured for eternity, like those purple mountain majesties.

Hardly. While the schools don't teach it, the establishment media avoids mentioning it, and most Americans haven't questioned it until recently, here's the far grittier reality: *Middle-class life in our country is not a given.*

The forty-hour week, a minimum-wage floor, collective bargaining for workers, affordable housing and cheap home loans, free education, the GI Bill, some retirement security for everyone, Medicare, job-safety protections, and so much more are what sustains the middle-class possibility for a majority of our people. These were not provided by the founders in 1776, and they certainly were not given to us by generous corporate chieftains. Rather, the middle-class framework was built by us . . . We the People.

In the first century of our republic, there was very little in the way of a middle class. But in the intervening decades, ordinary working stiffs agitated, organized, and literally battled the bosses, politicians, and media until, piece by piece, over the generations, we put into law the provisions that have given us a modicum of control over our own livelihoods and economic destinies.

But now, piece by piece, the bosses and politicians are rapidly dismantling this middle-class framework. We've seen pieces of this theft: the looting of our public treasury through tax giveaways to the rich; the White House assault on regulatory protections for everything from workplace safety to health care; the high-tech industry's despicable manipulation of immigration loopholes to displace middle-class American employees; the privatization push through every agency of government; the secretly negotiated trade deals that empower global corporations to subjugate workers throughout the world; the maneuvering to gut the pension laws so corporations can evade their legal and moral obligations to retirees . . . and so many more.

PAY HIKES

Congress and the White House refuse even to discuss raising America's wage floor, even though our miserly $5.15-an-hour minimum wage (that's a gross pay of $11,000 a year for full-time work) has not been raised since 1997.

Yet in five of the past six years since then, our Congress critters have raised the wages of a special group of American employees: themselves! Asked about these do-it-yourself pay raises, GOP Majority Leader Tom DeLay snapped:

"I challenge anyone to live on my salary."

He's paid $166,700 a year.

Last year's ruling on overtime pay by Bush's antilabor department is an example of how they're removing the legal infrastructure that supports a middle-class life. It lets corporations arbitrarily designate millions of wage workers as "managerial" employees, thus exempting them from overtime pay. Such workers as nurses, firefighters, and computer programmers will be forced to work more hours for no pay—taking money out of their pockets, stealing their weekends . . . and stealing their right to a life beyond the job.

The whole of this theft adds up to far worse than the sum of its parts, for it is America's egalitarian ethic of the common good that they are abandoning. It is said that the rich and poor will always be with us. Perhaps. But it is not assured anywhere or in any generation that the middle class will be with us.

As was true in the construction of our middle-class framework, its continued existence is dependent on ordinary folks like us standing up to those who're now so determined to dismantle it.

Bush Creates New Manufacturing Jobs!

I have excellent news, Americans! The Bushites have come up with a surefire plan to increase the number of manufacturing jobs in the USA! And you thought they didn't care.

Yes, while Democrats merely complain about the demise of such jobs and criticize U.S. corporations that are callously abandoning our middle class, George W and his team are stepping forward with creative, can-do solutions that, I think, can only be described as astonishing.

Their plan is proposed in the fine print of the voluminous "Economic Report of the President," issued in February. The suggestion by George W's top economists is that the hundreds of thousands of people who work in such fast-food joints as McDonald's and Subway are really not part of the service economy, but more accurately should be reclassified as manufacturing workers, just as those who make cars and other industrial products. After all, contend Bush's crack team of job classifiers, when you insert that meat patty, lettuce, cheese, and ketchup into a sliced bun, you are engaged in the combining of inputs to "manufacture" a product, no less so than those who assemble electronic parts to manufacture, say, a computer.

Bush's innovative economists also note that manufacturing is officially defined as "the mechanical, physical, or chemical transformation of materials into new products," and, they claim, when you heat ground beef, you are, in fact, chemically transforming it into a burger.

Of course, if Bush can redefine all those hamburger flippers as manufacturing workers, then he can statistically hush the critics who've been pointing to the drastic decline in these production jobs. There's another upside for the Bushites, too: Since manufacturing gets special tax breaks, suddenly Bush's backers in the fast-food industry serendipitously qualify.

But I'm not criticizing—hell, I'm with Bush on this one. After all, by assembling nouns, verbs, adjectives, and whatnot, I have manufactured this piece, and by applying the chemistry of my tiny brain cells, I have transformed raw words into a new product of sentences and paragraphs. Manufacturers of the world, unite! Now, where do I go to get my tax break?

Happy Days Are Here Again

Hallelujah and hosanna, shout the Little Rosy Scenarios in the White House, hailing 2004's rise in corporate profits and the stock market. George himself bleats regularly and loudly that "America's economy is strong and getting stronger," and this year's "Economic Report of the President" was even more bullish, flat-out predicting that 2.6 million jobs will be created. The boom is back, they exult!

Uh-huh, say the people out here in the real world, asking wearily: "A boom for whom?" Indeed, Bush's 2003 economic report predicted that 1.7 million jobs would be created last year, thanks to his tax cuts for the wealthy. He was off a bit. The nation actually *lost* jobs. Bush is on track to be the first president since Herbert "I don't see no Depression" Hoover to end his term with America having fewer jobs than when he took office. Bush's promise of massive job growth this year is so laugh-out-loud absurd that

She's the Secretary of What?

On the day it was announced that the monthly job report for January was far more anemic than expected, thus continuing the woes of America's working families, labor secretary Elaine Chao was perkily upbeat, offering the silver-lining perspective of Wall Street:

"Well, the stock market is, after all, the final arbiter [of the economy's health]. And the stock market was very strong this morning in reaction to the news that we have just received."

even his own treasury and commerce secretaries blush and run away when asked about it.

Smiley-faced statistics can't cover up the harsh job reality faced by most folks these days—a reality of no work, poverty work, or overwork.

Start with no work. Nearly 9 million Americans are officially unemployed. This doesn't include those who are so discouraged by the debilitating search for work that they've given up looking—they simply don't get counted. Neither do those who might get a one-day odd job during the month—they're actually treated as being fully "employed." Nor does it count those who bravely insist that they're now "self-employed," yet they have no paying work. It also doesn't count those who are working part-time but need a full-time job, or those who've only been temporarily hired for, say, retail sales during a holiday season and will be let go right after the holiday.

Then there's poverty work. These are the millions who've been Wal-Marted—technically they have jobs, but the pay is so low they live in poverty, with no health care, pension, or job security. More and more industries—from service to high tech—are saying that this is America's work future. Get used to it, they say.

Which leaves us with overwork. This includes those of you who have to take two or three low-paying jobs, working days and nights just to cover your bills, as well as those working in downsized com-

GEORGE GOES PICNICKING

Last year, with public anxiety over joblessness spreading as fast as, well, joblessness, Bush's political plotters had the brilliant idea of plopping him down at a Pennsylvania Labor Day picnic. Labor Day . . . Bush—a classic oxymoron. This son of wealth, a corporate guy, the most antilabor president since Labor Day itself was created, looked about as natural at that picnic as a goose wearing a tuxedo.

Nonetheless, it gave George a setting to reveal what the advance press notice promised would be a major new presidential initiative for "bringing back blue-collar jobs." Bush tried to rally the crowd (perhaps harkening back to his cheerleader days at Yale) by yelling out: "Things are getting better." No applause . . . murmurs. Then he cheerfully noted that worker productivity was up. Again, no applause—perhaps no one told him that increased productivity means fewer jobs for workers. So then he decided to go ahead and drop his bombshell of a jobs initiative on the crowd, announcing that—ta da!—he was creating a brand-new government position: assistant secretary of commerce for manufacturing.

You can imagine the excitement that caused.

panies with too few employees to do the work, meaning you have to work longer hours and on weekends. Balk . . . and you get the boot.

Forget what politicians and economists say—we'll know there's a real recovery when everyone has a good job at good wages with good benefits. Everything else is a lie.

The Statistically Employed

The next time you hear another news report or politician gushing about new jobs being created, think about Stan Malabey in Tucson, Arizona.

Mr. Malabey has one of those "jobs." He's one of the hundreds of thousands of Americans who do day labor. They scramble down to some hiring hall way before dawn each morning, huddling in the dark and hoping to be one of the few who'll be chosen to work at minimum wage for a few hours that day, literally doing the heavy lifting for homebuilders, landscapers, and the like.

Day laborers like Malabey are mostly hired through such corporate chains as Labor Ready, one of the largest in the country. The *Arizona Daily Star* reports that Labor Ready rounds up the workers (many of whom are homeless), hauls them in a van to and from the work site, then pays them about $5.15 an hour at the end of a hard day's work. Labor Ready reaps a tidy profit by charging the contractor for each worker it provides, then squeezing every dime it can from the workers.

For example, before they even leave the hiring hall, the workers are charged $2 each for a pair of work gloves. The van ride costs each of them another $3. Then, rather than paying in cash, Labor Ready gives the workers a company voucher, which they have to redeem at the company's cash machines. The machines subtract another $1.50 fee from the workers' pay vouchers. As one worker said about the van ride, "Three bucks might not sound like a lot of money, but it's a lot of money to me." And Malabey adds: "The work is hard, and you want every little dime you can get."

By squeezing those dimes from the workers, Labor Ready makes a killing. The *Star* found that $5 million of the corporation's $23 million in profits in 1999 came from those cash machines.

Politicians get to count the Stan Malabeys of our country as another digit of economic success. These people are, after all, statistically employed, thus fulfilling political promises to "Get America Working!" There are millions of these people doing hard work in everything from poultry plants to Wal-Marts, drawing poverty pay. But these aren't jobs. More like jobettes. If a company can't pay a real wage and treat workers with fairness and common human decency, then it hasn't really created a job, and the richest country in the world should not be counting them as such.

CEOs Average $25,000 . . . an Hour

A national magazine recently featured a story about the paychecks of corporate CEOs. The cover featured a pink-faced pig dressed in a business suit, and the title said it all: "Oink!" The magazine bluntly labeled today's executive class "a symbol of cartoonish greed," asking in exasperation, "Have they no shame?"

The significance of this article is that it was not the cover story of some lefty rag, but the April 14 issue of *Fortune,* the very bible of CEO-dom! Even some of the in-house set are astonished by the audacious avarice of America's top corporate leaders, gaping openmouthed at the miserable moral example of CEOs continuing to practice the imperious ethic of "I."

These thieves in Guccis are grabbing all they can for themselves at a time when millions of workers are being dumped, pensioners are ripped off, unemployment is skyrocketing, college graduates are trading mortarboards for hairnets, and the general economy is rolling into the ditch.

Apparently born without the blush gene, top CEOs and their apologists have resorted to old-fashioned flimflam to divert public and political attention from their looting. With the laudable exception of *Fortune*, most of the media establishment (itself headed by such grossly overpaid execs as Michael Eisner at Disney-owned ABC) would have us believe that CEOs have now seen the light, trimmed their excess, and begun to share the sacrifice of a down economy. "The days of the fantasyland CEO pay package appear to be in the past," trumpeted *BusinessWeek* in a typical comment.

Yet if you're like me, you might think that $50 million for a year's work still qualifies as fantasyland. That's the average haul in 2002 for the twenty top-paid chiefs listed by *BusinessWeek,* including several who drove their companies straight into bankruptcy, sank their shareholders' stock value to worthless levels, and presently are under criminal investigation.

Fortune points out that far from coming down to earth, the median pay for CEOs at one hundred of the largest corporations rose by 14 percent. Meanwhile, the performance of corporate stocks fell by 23 percent, and overall wages and benefits for employees barely kept up with inflation.

Take the fellow mentioned earlier—Michael Eisner of Disney, Inc. *Forbes* magazine has just designated him the very worst performing CEO of the past six years, having produced a nearly 5 percent loss for shareholders while pocketing an average of $122 million a year in personal pay.

The performance by Disney's chief Mouseketeer was so poor that in both 2000 and 2001 he failed to meet the company's criteria for earning a bonus, but in 2003—*bingo!*—he got a $5 million bonus. Had his performance improved? No. He simply had his board of directors lower the requirements for him to "earn" a bonus.

Wait . . . aren't these corporate directors supposed to be the

HOLIDAY CHEER

December 2003 holiday sales were in the ditch, even at discount outfits like Wal-Mart. The one exception to this glum trend was at your high-end stores, such as Neiman Marcus, Tiffany, and Saks Fifth Avenue.

The CEO of Neiman Marcus exulted that holiday shoppers in his swank stores "proved that luxury is alive." Indeed, sales of such stocking stuffers as $5,000 to $10,000 watches were up 16 percent this season over last! There were similar jumps in diamonds, gold, and cashmere goods, and Neiman reported that sales of Chanel, Prada, and Gucci handbags were "absolutely miraculous."

And why not, dears? After all, this is the crowd that took the bulk of Bush's tax giveaways. While a typical family might have gotten a $400 tax cut, if they were lucky, the millionaire families averaged $93,000 each in cuts. That'll buy a lot of baubles and gewgaws.

overseers of CEOs, the shareholders' watchdog, the people's stop-gap against excess? Ha! Boards have become brother-in-law deals, with the members commonly handpicked by the CEO and lavishly rewarded for attending a couple of meetings a year to rubber-stamp whatever the CEO proposes.

Most boards are made up of other CEOs, all of whom are golfing buddies and sit on one another's boards. It's an insider game in which they wink and take care of each other's puffed-up paychecks. "It's sort of like the Golden Rule gone wrong," observes a Harvard professor of business.

What we have here are people who must be snorting undiluted hubris two or three times a day, giving them a constant high that makes them feel entitled to any excess. CEOs treat all other employees as disposable units, but they see themselves as The Source, the irreplaceable fount of genius from which corporate success

> **Did I mention that BOSS spelled backward is double-SOB?**

flows. In their minds, such rare genius cannot be rewarded enough.

So even after the greed-induced collapse of the Enrons and WorldComs, even after the embarrassment of Tyco spending $6,000 to buy a shower curtain for its CEO ($6,000! Could you ever let it get wet?), and even after they've destroyed trust and sowed suspicion throughout the workplace, destroying the ethos of egalitarianism that is essential to a democratic society—these executives still don't get it, and are continuing to separate their personal enrichment from the common good.

Clearly these guys are out of control, and it's time for an intervention to save them (and us shareholders, workers et al.) from a total CEO pig-out.

What to do? Aha . . . I've got it! Since our corporate chieftains are endlessly extolling the virtues of global free-market policies to workers, Third World nations, environmentalists, and everyone else, what say we give them a little pinch of globalism?

CEOs say they shouldn't be bound by borders and have to pay U.S. wages or U.S. taxes. So here's the question: Why should we be bound by U.S. CEOs? Just as they've been able to roam the globe in search of the cheapest labor possible (currently in Vietnam at a nickel an hour, unless you count China's prison labor, which is "free"), so should we go a-roamin' for cheaper execs.

The average top executive in our country grabs five hundred times more in pay than the typical hourly employee in the same company. Compare this 500-to-1 ratio with those in countries competing with us in the global market, as reported by *Business Week:*

Brazil	57 to 1
Mexico	45 to 1
Hong Kong	38 to 1
Britain	25 to 1

Australia	22 to 1
China	21 to 1
Italy	19 to 1
Spain	18 to 1
France	16 to 1
Taiwan	16 to 1
Germany	11 to 1
South Korea	11 to 1
Japan	10 to 1

So come on, you executive search committees, start thinking outside the box and apply a little global competition to the executive suite! Today's princely CEOs say that their bloated paychecks are simply a product of what the market will bear. It's time to broaden the market.

Just as U.S. companies are routinely bringing in software programmers from India and agricultural workers from Central America to lower the pay scales in these industries, so can they import some skilled executives from Brazil, Italy, or Japan who'll work for a tenth or less of what our spoiled CEO workforce is getting.

We could create a special executive immigration program called something snappy, like ExecExpress, and instead of green cards issue them platinum cards. We'll get those astronomical pay packages down to earth in no time, the old-fashioned way: market magic.

Converting Safeway to Greedway

Corporate greed is not some amorphous concept, but a human characteristic that comes with faces and names—such as Steven Burd.

He's CEO of Safeway, the sprawling supermarket giant. Burd recently led the five-month charge in California to bust the wage scale and eliminate the health-care benefits of his industry's employees.

Supermarket work won't make you a millionaire, but thanks to the United Food and Commercial Workers Union (UFCW), employees who are unionized can earn a slice of America's middle-class life. In California, baggers and clerks start at about $7.50 an hour and rise to about $18. It's this rise to the middle class that Burd and his corporate buddies targeted for eventual elimination, claiming that it's no longer financially feasible for corporations to sustain such pay, health care, and other middle-class standards.

Even though this industry's profits were up 91 percent since 1998, including $10 billion in profits in 2002, executives had been whacking at workers' earnings for some time. For example, $18 an hour produces an income of about $36,000 a year for full-time work. But grocery executives have been holding workers to between twenty-four and thirty-two hours a week—cutting their annual earnings to around $25,000—or less.

Even that was too much for Burd, however. As Safeway's contract with UFCW was coming up for renewal in 2003, he demanded that their pay be frozen for two years, that their health-care

EVERY DAY IN AMERICA . . .

85,444 workers lose their jobs.

14.7 *million* workers are jobless, underemployed, or have given up looking for work.

43.6 *million* people have no health insurance.

4,227 people file for personal bankruptcy.

12,878 workers are injured or made ill by their jobs.

6.8 *million* people are in the workforce but still poor.

Source: "Jobs: AFL-CIO Special Report" (March 2004)

benefits be slashed, and that new employees be hired at a drastically lowered pay scale. This was Wal-Martization, and UFCW members balked. Safeway refused to negotiate, however, forcing its longtime workers to go out on strike last October.

Anyone who thinks labor unions strike just for the hell of it has never been in one. It's financially and emotionally draining. But there was no choice here. As one of the workers put it: "If we lose this fight, there goes seventy thousand jobs that will no longer be middle-class jobs."

He was talking about the jobs of twenty thousand Safeway employees in southern California, plus fifty thousand more supermarket workers in the region who were locked out of their jobs by Kroger and Albertsons only one day after the Safeway strike began. Can you say "anticompetitive collusion"?

The hardships endured by these workers were staggering. For nearly half a year, they struggled without any unemployment compensation or health coverage, and strike benefits paid only $125 a week. Many lost their apartments and cars because they couldn't make the rent or keep up with the payments. The stress on them was enormous, taking a toll on their health and their families.

The supermarkets were eating big losses, too, for California consumers rallied behind the workers and sought out other grocers for their food purchases. But the top executives continued to draw their fat salaries (Burd is paid $7 million a year) and enjoy the Rolls-Royce of health coverage, so they refused any serious negotiation, even when the union offered a major concession that would have saved the corporations a third of a billion dollars on their employees' health plans. The CEOs were not interested in compromise, they wanted it all. Burd cynically said that breaking the living standard of his own employees was an "investment in the future" of Safeway, by which he meant that the company could gain fat profits down the road by having a poverty-level workforce. It was an investment in people's misery.

Another reason the top dogs thought they could stall and effectively starve out the workers was that Safeway, Kroger, and Albertsons had entered into a mutual-aid pact weeks before the strike began, agreeing not to compete, to share costs and revenues, and to act in unison against their workers. The state attorney general filed an antitrust suit against the three, but corporate lawyers kept it stuck in the courts while the workers suffered.

This was not merely a dispute about seventy thousand California workers but part of a national class war about whether corporations everywhere can simply reduce all of us to low-wage, no benefit work. If Safeway succeeded here, the entire retailing industry would push for the same Wal-Mart model, knocking America's majority further down.

But Burd and his corporate confederates made one miscalculation: They underestimated the determination, unity, and endurance of their employees. They thought the financial pressure on workers' families would be so great that union members would cave in after two or three months. But it became the longest grocery strike in U.S. history, going twice as long as the industry assumed, with workers stretching themselves and their families beyond what anyone thought possible. The chains had lost $1.5 billion in revenues in the five months, but the CEOs had their collusion going for them, the still-deep pockets of their national companies, and a brutish, red-faced, driving determination to crush the industry's pay scale, hoping to jack up the corporations' stock prices and walk away with more for themselves.

The end came on Leap Year's Day, February 29, when UFCW members voted overwhelmingly to accept a new company offer and go back to work. The union took a big hit, swallowing a provision that allows the chains to hire new employees at reduced pay and with reduced benefits. Yet the chains were not able to knock down the pay of current workers or to achieve their key goal in the forced strike, which was to slash the workers' health-care benefits. The intended knockout blow to middle-class grocery jobs was fended off by the fortitude of these workers who were willing to make a stand . . . and a sacrifice.

This is a war that has only begun. The Steven Burds of every industry will keep attacking, keep trying to take back more from America's workers. But a growing majority of working folks are at last becoming aware that it's all of us who are targeted, and that the nature of the assault is not merely about some jobs over here or some benefits over there; it's about whether or not America will be a middle-class country. That's a war we have to fight, a war that's worthy of our best efforts.

The energy and awareness unleashed by those seventy thousand workers will roll across our land for years to come.

Bush's PR Boo-Boo

George W's handlers are masters of the presidential photo op, posing their boy just perfectly to convey a positive message for the TV cameras.

But Bush's puffers and buffers boo-booed badly in St. Louis last year. George had been flown in to make a political sales pitch for his tax-cut plan to help the superrich. To cast this multibillion-dollar giveaway in a soft, warm, and fuzzy "populist" light, his handlers chose the warehouse of a St. Louis trucking company as their press conference setting. It seemed perfectly suited to make us think that his program is all about helping small businesses in the heartland to create jobs for America. Don't think of it as a tax cut, was the spin, think of it as a grassroots plan to revitalize our sagging economy.

So there was George as the cameras rolled, giving his speech in front of what appeared to be stacks of cardboard boxes ready to move out. Only, there were no real boxes in the picture. Instead, he spoke in front of a canvas backdrop painted to look like boxes

> **" There are four or five times as many smart, driven people in China than there are in the U.S. "**
>
> **—Alan Lacey, CEO of Sears, planning to send technology jobs offshore**

and bearing the proud, bold letters: "Made in America."

Why the faux prop, why not use the real boxes that were stacked all around the warehouse? Because, at the eleventh hour, the Bushites discovered that the actual boxes were plainly stamped for all to see: "Made in China."

Oops. This was definitely off message. The spin of the day was that Bush's tax scheme for the rich would trickle down to Made-in-America jobs—not more imports from China. This was not good. OK, said the handlers, we can put George over here in front of a painted backdrop, but still, this place will be crawling with reporters. What'll we do to keep them from seeing the real boxes?

That's when Bush workers were given rolls of duct tape to go through the whole warehouse, literally covering up the "Made in China" markings on each box. But let's look on the positive side: Bush found yet another use for duct tape. Is that stuff still made in America?

Bush's Jobs Plan

In his January State of the Union peroration, George "Pinocchio" Bush's biggest lie was not about weapons of mass destruction.

Attempting to diffuse the growing anxiety and anger about the loss of middle-class jobs, he made the bald-faced assertion that the solution is simple: more job training. Millions of unemployed and underemployed Americans must have stared in slack-jawed disbelief as this son of privilege mouthed the corporate line that everything is OK with our economy, *if only America's worthless workers would get more training and improve their skills.*

DID YOU KNOW?

OF IMPORTS INTO THE U.S., CHINA ACCOUNTS FOR:

95 percent of stuffed toys

88 percent of radios

87 percent of Christmas trees, wreaths, and ornaments

83 percent of toys

70 percent of leather goods

67 percent of shoes

67 percent of handbags

65 percent of lamps and lights

64 percent of cases for cameras, eyeglasses, etc.

60 percent of drills and power tools

57 percent of line telephones

56 percent of household plastics

54 percent of sporting goods

53 percent of ceramic kitchenware

27 percent of wooden furniture

ALSO:

The $100 Game Boy Advance?

The $89 Sony CD/DVD Player?

The $30 Meade Infinity Microscope/Telescope?

The $18 Nickelodeon SpongeBob SquarePants Skateboard?

The $9 Disney Baby Tigger doll?

(China, China, China, China, and China)

BONUS FACTOID

Wal-Mart is the world's largest importer of products made in China.

Training for what? Here came George's whopper: "Much of our job growth will be found in high-skilled fields." That's a lie and Bush knows it. Well, OK, he's clueless about real life, so he probably doesn't know it, but his speechwriters do.

Bush's own Labor Department reports that of the thirty occupations that will account for the highest job growth between now and 2010, two thirds require minimal skills. High-tech companies will create only 284,000 more jobs for computer software engineers in that period—while ten times more jobs than that will be created in just these seven very low-tech fields: freight movers, home health aides, janitors, waitresses, security guards, office clerks, and cashiers. The number one job-creator for America's future? Restaurant workers, including fast food. This category alone will create ten times more jobs than will software engineering. You don't need a high-tech degree, you need a hairnet! And all of these jobs pay pitiful wages—of the top thirty "growth jobs," nearly half pay only $14,000 to $20,000 a year.

By the way, despite his call for more training in each of his four years, Bush has cut the budgets of our federal job-training programs. And forget about getting one of those 284,000 software engineering jobs—companies are now shipping them off to India, Russia, and other low-wage countries.

Training doesn't create jobs, and low-wage jobs don't create a middle class. America needs a living wage, labor law reform, an end to subsidies for corporations that ship our good jobs out . . . and a president who has a clue.

High-Tech Execs to Workers: Go to Hell

Remember how we were told that globalization would be such a boon for American workers? Blue collar was going to become white collar, low wage would move up to high tech, and everyone would sing zippity-doo-dah all the day long!

AMERICA'S HIGH-TECH FUTURE!

(Jobs with the largest growth between now and 2010)

JOB	ANNUAL PAY	EDUCATION LEVEL
1. Food preparer	$16,000	On-the-job training
2. Customer service rep.	$26,000	On-the-job training
3. Registered nurse	$48,000	Two-year degree
4. Retail sales clerk	$18,000	On-the-job training
5. Computer support specialist	$39,000	Two-year degree
6. Cashier	$15,000	On-the-job training
7. Office clerk	$22,000	On-the-job training
8. Security guard	$19,000	On-the-job training
9. Computer technician	$55,000	Bachelor's degree
10. Waiter/waitress	$14,000	On-the-job training
11. General manager	$68,000	Bachelor's degree
12. Truck driver	$33,000	On-the-job training
13. Nursing aide	$19,000	On-the-job training
14. Janitor	$18,000	On-the-job training
15. College teachers	$52,000	Doctoral degree
16. Teacher assistant	$19,000	On-the-job training
17. Home health aide	$18,000	On-the-job training
18. Freight hauler	$19,000	On-the-job training
19. Computer engineer	$70,000	Bachelor's degree
20. Landscaping worker	$20,000	On-the-job training
21. Personal and home care aide	$16,000	On-the-job training
22. Computer analyst	$63,000	Bachelor's degree
23. Receptionist	$21,000	On-the-job training
24. Delivery truck driver	$24,000	On-the-job training
25. Hand packager	$16,000	On-the-job training
26. Elementary school teacher	$42,000	Bachelor's degree
27. Medical assistant	$24,000	On-the-job training
28. Database administration	$55,000	Bachelor's degree
29. Secondary school teacher	$43,000	Bachelor's degree
30. Auditor	$47,000	Bachelor's degree

Source: Bureau of Labor Statistics

They were feeding us globaloney. Dell, Microsoft, IBM, Google, Oracle, Intel, CSC, and the other greedheaded giants of high tech are swiftly moving these very jobs out of our country to China, India, Pakistan, Russia, and elsewhere, making a killing by paying a fourth as much to a foreign employee as they pay here, then pocketing the difference.

This is leading to a tense workplace. Internal IBM memos show that while U.S. companies are ecstatic about the bucks they gain by abandoning the homeland, they're very skittish about the anger this engenders. One of the memos tells top managers to be evasive when talking about the company's long-range employment plans, advising them that "Terms 'on-shore' and 'off-shore' should never be used," and that anything written to employees must first be "sanitized" by the corporate communications department.

IBM says it'll "save" $168 million in 2004 by replacing three thousand of its "knowledge workers" with cheaper versions abroad. These are the jobs that were supposed to represent the future of upward mobility in America, but instead, the "global sourcing" of such work (as IBM's fun-loving corporate jargon-meisters call it) is leading to a distressing wave of downward mobility in our country.

"Think India . . . pick something to move offshore today."

—Microsoft executive to department heads, 2002

IBM now provides a "suggested script" for managers faced with telling employees that their jobs are going bye-bye. For example, to soften the blow, managers are instructed to say: "This action is a statement about the rate and pace of change in this demanding industry. . . . It is in no way a comment on the excellent work you have done over the years." That's a bit like slathering some Oil of Olay on the stiletto you're thrusting into someone's back.

L IS FOR LOOPHOLE

Such corporations as Cigna, GE, and Merrill Lynch have been using an obscure provision in our nation's immigration laws to import low-wage technology workers from India to replace Americans.

Called the L-1 visa, it was devised for occasional use by U.S. firms needing to transfer a few key foreign employees to the home branch. But the corporations are now driving an immigration truck through the L-1 loophole, having brought some 325,000 high-tech workers into our country in the last year or so, mostly from India. These skilled people are hired by Indian-based recruitment firms, then shipped wholesale through the L-1 loophole to America, where technically they are employed by the U.S. branches of the recruitment firms. But these firms do no high-tech work. They're essentially temp companies that hire out the Indian visa-holders to U.S. corporations, which pay them a third to a half less than the Americans they replace. It's common for the corporations to require outgoing U.S. workers to train the L-1 workers who'll be given their jobs.

Bush has not supported efforts to plug this loophole.

The official corporate line, repeated religiously by politicians and pundits, is that high tech is such a zoom-zoom industry that a discarded worker can easily and quickly find another job. They might check with Mary Lowrance about that. She was a high-tech worker for AMD Corporation, where she'd won awards for setting production records and helping devise ways for the company to save money. AMD repaid her by sending her job offshore. A year and a half later, she's still out of work, even after applying to more than five hundred other firms. "My job has gone away," she says. "There are just no jobs to be had."

To add insult to injury, many American high-tech workers are forced to train their foreign replacements! Refuse, and they lose any severance pay.

Even some Republican leaders, such as Representative Don Manzullo of Illinois, are gagging on this globaloney: "The assumption was that while lower-skilled jobs would be done elsewhere, it would allow Americans to focus on higher-skilled, higher-paying opportunities. But what do you tell the Ph.D. or professional engineer or architect or accountant or computer scientist to do next. Where do you tell them to go?"

If you're a high-tech CEO, you tell 'em to go to hell.

Get to Work, America

Congratulations, Americans . . . you're number one!

Not only are you a repeat winner, but you people keep extending your lead over your nearest competitors. Yessiree, no other industrial nation in the world can touch us Americans when it comes to putting in long hours on the job.

On average, U.S. workers are now at their tasks for a total of nearly two thousand hours a year—or about fifty weeks. That's up thirty-six hours since 1990, meaning we're now averaging almost a full week more at work each year than we did then. That literally beats the work pants off the Japanese, who were the world's number one workaholics until we toppled them in the mid-nineties. Now we're working three and a half weeks per year longer than the Japanese, six and a half weeks longer than the British, and twelve and a half weeks longer than the Germans.

Those softies have fallen behind in the work race because they've built their economy around the concept of citizens getting more time to recharge their batteries, be with their families, broaden themselves with vacations and sabbaticals, and—get this—*enjoy life.* Ha! What a bunch of slackers.

And while they're lollygagging around on vacation for a month, six weeks, or more, we're typically on the job fifty out of fifty-two weeks a year. Our ulcers are bigger than any of those foreigners' ulcers, by golly!

America has jumped to the top of the work heap because those in charge in Washington and on Wall Street have built our economy around stagnant wages and constant downsizings, prompting our people to keep their noses to the grindstone, work extra hours, avoid unionizing, and take two or three jobs to make ends meet. Way to go! I'll bet you're just busting with pride to be at the top in terms of hours worked, even if we're at the bottom in terms of income paid, compared with the Japanese, British, Germans, and other industrial competitors.

Still, we Americans can't rest on our laurels—in fact, we don't rest at all. Let's break that two-thousand-hour-a-year barrier! Come on, people, we can do it. Maybe you could get a part-time job on Sundays instead of goofing off like you've been doing.

Gifts to Power

I want to offer gifts to the people in power in our nation. Let me start with our Congress critters. To each one I send my fondest wish that from now on they receive the exact same income, pay increases, health care, and pensions that we average citizens get. If they get only the American average, my guess is that this will enrich their lives by making them a bit more humble—and a whole lot more eager to serve the public's needs.

For America's CEOs, my gift is a beautifully boxed, brand-new set of corporate ethics. It's an elegant yet simple set, called the golden rule: "Do unto others as you would have them do unto you." Going to pollute someone's neighborhood? Then you have to live there, too. Going to slash wages and benefits? Then slash yours as well. Going to move your manufacturing to sweatshops in

China? Then put your office right inside the worst of those sweat-shops. Executive life won't be as luxurious, but you'll enjoy a new purity of spirit.

There are a few special people on my list, too. For George W. Bush, who likes to pose for the TV cameras as a brush-clearing ranch hand on his ranchette in Crawford, Texas, I send my deepest hope that, after this November, he'll be free to clear brush full-time! Imagine the fun he'll have, and he won't be bothered by those TV crews watching him do it.

For Democratic leaders in Congress, I've sent jumbo glue-guns filled with Elmer's Super Glue in the hope that they'll inject each other's vertebrae to stiffen their spines so they can start standing up to Bush and the moneyed elites.

Finally, I got a doll for Tom DeLay of Texas, the power-mad GOP majority leader. Only, he doesn't get the doll—I keep it. It's a voodoo doll of Tom himself, and I'll stick pins into it every time this vindictive, vituperative, right-wing political extremist starts getting nasty again. I jab a pin in the doll's head and Tom's hair catches on fire. It'll make him a better person.

A Big Idea

What if the White House and Congress were to do something sensible, positive, visionary, and good for everyone, instead of . . . well, you know, the opposite of all of the above, as they've been doing?

Here's one big idea that would definitely be a plus for our people and for future generations: launch a ten-year, $300 billion crash program to provide energy independence for America. This would be a nationwide effort involving millions of us grassroots people to develop, build, and run a high-speed rail network, a distribution system for hydrogen-powered cars, energy-efficient buildings and appliances, solar- and wind-power systems, and other means to kick our nation's costly oil addiction.

It's called the Apollo Project, and it's a proposal that has been put together by ten unions, including the Steelworkers, Auto Workers, Mine Workers, Service Employees, Machinists, and Electrical Workers. Among other good results, their bold plan can restore America's manufacturing jobs, link blue-collar America with the environmental movement, eliminate the need for more oil wars, build a sound energy infrastructure for the future, spur a national construction boom, stimulate the economy from the ground up, excite and unite workaday Americans in a shared mission, and provide a positive model for the rest of the world.

Now that's sensible, positive, visionary, and good for everyone!

Froodle-doodle, cry the naysayers in the White House, Congress, and oil corporations, where are you going to get $300 billion to finance this? I say we should get it from where it went. Last year, in one tax cut alone, Washington doled out $350 billion from our public treasury, mostly to enrich elites who were already super-rich. Let's put $300 billion of that back in the treasury to finance this Apollo program for the good of all, instead of watching the privileged stick it in foreign bank accounts or buy more foreign villas.

A Corporation That Breaks the Greed Mold

Do big-time CEOs, no matter how compassionate and cuddly they might be personally, have to be SOBs on the job?

Yes, says the conventional wisdom of greater CorporateWorld. The imperative of the bottom line dictates that wages and benefits be slashed and that offshoring be pursued with a vengeance. It's not personal, just business, the inevitable workings of the market, they say.

"Look ye to Wal-Mart," boom the market gods, directing CEOs to follow the antilabor, low-wage, no benefit, move-it-all-to-China ethic of this giant. The gods decree that no one can outcompete Wal-Mart, so best to imitate the beast.

Apparently, Jim Sinegal has been going to the wrong church. He's CEO of Costco, the warehouse club retailer that's fast spreading across the country. He takes a shockingly heretical view of his job, boasting of his company's fair treatment of employees: "We pay much better than Wal-Mart," Sinegal says. "That's not altruism. It's good business."

> **"If you hire good people, give them good jobs, and pay them good wages, generally something good is going to happen."**
> —*Jim Sinegal, CEO of Costco*

Indeed, Costco's pay is much, much, much better—a full-time Costco clerk or warehouse worker earns more than $41,000 a year, plus getting terrific health-care coverage. Wal-Mart workers get barely a third of that pay, plus a lousy health-care plan. Costco even has unions!

Yet Costco's total labor costs are only about half of Wal-Mart's. How's that possible? One big reason is that Costco workers feel valued and their morale is high, which adds enormously to the company's productivity. Also, they don't tend to leave—employee turnover is a tiny fraction of Wal-Mart's always revolving door, where total company turnover tops 50 percent a year! It's enormously expensive to be on a constant cycle of recruiting, training, and losing employees. Even a 10 percent reduction in employee turnover is said to produce a 20 percent saving on labor costs. Better to attract top-quality workers with decent pay . . . and keep them.

Another corporate maneuver Sinegal rejects is offshoring. Pointing to his company's U.S. call center, he says: "We could move it to Bangladesh or somewhere. But what kind of message would that send to our employees? Not a good one, I think."

One area where Wal-Mart does "better" is raking in the profits. By shortchanging workers, offshoring to China, squeezing suppliers, and forcing out local competitors, it is able to haul off about double the profit that Costco makes. Yet Costco is quite profitable in its own right, and shareholders can't really complain, since the value of their stock has risen 354 percent in the past ten years—way better than most corporations. Sinegal could wring more profit out of the company, but he believes that the better business model is to enjoy a nice profit, not a killing, while investing more of the company's resources in Costco's 92,000 workers. "I don't see what's wrong with an employee earning enough to be able to buy a house or having a health plan for the family," he says.

BUSHQUIZ

1. **What was George W's advice to our country after the September 11 terrorist attacks?**
   A. "Ask not what your country can do for you, but what you can do for your country."
   B. "Walk softly, but carry a big stick."
   C. "Go shopping."
   D. "The only thing we have to fear is fear itself."

2. **Who constructed the framework of the American middle class?**
   A. Halliburton
   B. The 1776 founders
   C. The Bill of Rights
   D. America's working stiffs

3. **The job reality faced by most folks today does *not* include which of the following?**
   A. No work
   B. Poverty work
   C. Overwork
   D. Dental work

4. **The president's Economic Roundtable believes that the best way to feed the birds is to:**
   A. Give the horses more oats
   B. Reclassify members of the avian class as manufacturing workers
   C. Force the little twits to work more hours
   D. All of the above

5. **Which of the following disasters is most likely to happen to a middle-class person this year?**
   A. A heart attack
   B. A terrorist attack
   C. A panic attack
   D. Bankruptcy

6. **Which of the following was George "Pinocchio" Bush's biggest lie of the year?**
   A. Iraq has weapons of mass destruction.
   B. Tax cuts for the rich help the working class.
   C. The solution to the loss of middle-class jobs is for workers to get training for high-tech jobs.
   D. The question is too difficult to answer.

7. **This skinflint CEO is proof that men don't have a monopoly on ruthlessness in offshoring American jobs:**
   A. Martha Stewart
   B. Christie Whitman
   C. Carly Fiorina
   D. Kathie Lee Gifford

8. **Which of the following could offer a big boost to the American economy for years to come?**
   A. Internet porn
   B. Higher CEO pay

C. The phenomenal growth of fast-food jobs

D. The Apollo Project

9. **By President Bush's new definition of "manufacturing," this company is the greatest manufacturing power in America:**

A. IBM

B. Ford

C. McDonald's

D. ExxonMobil

10. ***On the Job Fashion* magazine's recent "Careers of the Future" photo spread featured which of these hot and stylish occupational accessories:**

A. Hairnet

B. Security guard's gunbelt

C. Waiter/waitress's apron

D. All of the above

Answers on page 226.

3

One Word, Bucko: Yum-yum-yum!

☞ *Because of Bush's backing of corporations that are genetically altering our food supply, you'll soon be able to eat brussel sprouts that not only taste like bon-bons but also will have your heartburn medicine and erectile dysfunction pills genetically spliced into every bite.*

Yo, America—it's a Brave New World of food possibilities out there if only we dare to grab it! The beauty of Bush is that he's a natural let-it-be leader who instinctively understands that his role is to keep government from getting in the way of the grabbiteurs—the Monsantos, Tysons, Dows, ADMs, and other big-league food corporatizers, globalizers, and modifiers. They have the cojones, *cash, connections, clout, and—here's the big one:* vision!—*to do what's gotta be done.*

Now listen up. We've got a clear choice in 2004. America can vote to keep the business of agriculture in the gnarled hands of a bunch of Elmers trying to scratch out a living by working with fickle old Momma Nature, or we can get the hell outta Rubeville

and get into the with-it, high-tech, here-and-now third millennium that might not need soil, much less farmers, to make food—
and can make food do tricks that'd cause Elmer's eyes to explode.

I don't know about you, but I say we zip-zap the world's food
supply right into the corporate labs of the techno-knowhow boys,
into the modern factory model of agrocorporateculture, into the
comforting confines of America's conglomerate structure, where it
belongs, along with everything else that's serving us so well.

Yeah, yeah, yeah, you afraid-of-the-future sissies will always
throw up flack about "Ooooo, boo-hoo, what about the family
farm, what about rural towns, what about food being an organic
part of us?" Spare me. If you want bucolic, if you want natural,
make like a cow and graze on your lawn all day, but get outta my
face.

And don't even get me started about health and enviro screw-
balls who want everything tested before we turn it loose. The Bible
is clear on this. Did Noah test all the animals before he put 'em in
the ark? No, and thank God he didn't, or they'd all have drowned,
and we wouldn't have puppies to cuddle today. So get out of the
way of progress, you testacrats.

Speaking of puppies, don't you know what corporatizing food
production is all about? Compassion for children, that's what.
Sure, there are profits to be made, but the real motivation is that
Leave-No-Child-Behind, deeply personal compassion that George
and all the rest of us in the executive suites feel toward . . . the little ones. Pardon me if I get a little choked up here, but I for one
(and I know there are many others of you out there) know first-
hand about the trauma of being forced as a little tyke to eat lima
beans. Aaaulgcch! Nasty things made me gag.

Let's stop the torture of tykes. Let's make lima beans taste like
cheesecake! Happy smiles all around from the kids and their

hardworking, stressed-out parents who don't need a food fight at the end of their day. We could even splice a Valium into the limas. Don't you see? It's about puppies, children, and families—that's why we do all that we do.

It's part of George's endearing sweetness that he thinks like that, as opposed to your typical narcissistic family-hating, Democrat-leaning individuals, who don't ever want to unshackle corporate genius so it can be free of regulatory busybodies, free to help people.

Take world hunger. Liberals are always sobbing about the need to "share our abundance," wanting to send boatloads of grain to starving people. I guess they're too ignorant to recognize that grain is bulky, heavy, hard to ship. Instead of treating hunger with a farm product, here's a twenty-first-century, free-enterprise-in-action solution: pills!

You've got to look at the hunger population not as people but as a market, an opportunity for product innovation. They don't need food per se, they need nourishment, so let's turn loose Merck, Eli Lilly, Johnson & Johnson, and the other drug giants to engineer a mess of food pills. One little tablet a day will deliver all nutrition needs, the flavor-science technicians can make 'em taste like Thanksgiving dinner, and the hungry people won't even have to chew, just swallow.

George W gets it. The role of government is simply to give research and development money to the pharmaceutical companies, ban any lawsuits against unfortunate side effects of their products, buy the pills from the companies at their asking price and distribute them to the hungry, prevent any competition from Canada, China, or wherever—then get the hell out of the way so the free market can work.

Vision . . . that's what we need in a president.

M. WUERKER

GEORGE W DOES FOOD

Agriculture is a policy area that you'd expect our present president to know well, since he is widely known to be a rooty-toot-tootin' cow person. We know he is this, for the media is constantly reporting that Bush "will spend the month of August at his ranch," or that the prime minister of Upper Slobovia has been invited to meet with Bush at his ranch," or that "the thing the president seems happiest doing is cutting brush at his ranch."

The ranch has become a symbol of Bush the man, son of the soil. It's a large-scale version of those TV backdrops the White House puts behind him for presidential photo ops, repeating positive words over and over: Success . . . Bold . . . Fortitude . . . Trust . . . Compassion . . . Goofy . . . Vision . . . Integ . . . Wait! Who put Goofy up there? That's not on message. Karl! Kill somebody!

George's little spread outside of Crawford, Texas, is really not a ranch at all—more of a ranchette, a gentleman's hobby-place for playing rancher. Start with the curious fact that Crawford is actually farm country, not a ranching area. Bush only bought the place in 1999 after deciding to run for president, he doesn't actually ranch as a business, he only performs ranch-type work when national networks are there to cover it (and then only in short bursts), and it would be awfully good fun to see what "Rancher George" would do if a reporter asked him to demonstrate a real rancher chore, such as artificially inseminating a cow.

Then there's that hat. He likes to wear his cowboy hat when talking to the media at the ranchette, and it's a perfect Stetson. Way too perfect. It has to be a $1,000 headpiece (probably picked up at Neiman Marcus) and it's always spotless, like it just came out of the box. Real ranchers don't ranch in $1,000 hats. Also, a cowboy hat isn't real unless its got some creases, notches, and several blotches of dirt, blood, beer, and barbecue sauce here and there.

Like my ol' momma used to say: "You can put a sack of sand in the oven, but it won't turn out biscuits." [**Author's Admission:** Actually, Momma's a classy lady who never said any such thing, but I've always wanted to use that line, and well, I needed somebody to say it; besides, it fits well here.]

Karl Rove can put George on a ranchy-looking place, but that doesn't make him a rancher. And as you can see from the food and farm policies that Bush pushes—everything from his $17-billion-a-year farm program to his head-in-the-BS approach to mad cow disease—far from being a jeans-and-boots guy, George is every bit the pinstripe-and-wingtips corporatist. He has sided consistently with global middlemen, genetic manipulators, pesticide makers, meat contaminators, factory-farm operators, and other corporate interests against small producers, organics, consumers, nature . . . and common sense.

Down on the Farm

Bush raised the corporate flag over the U.S. Department of Agriculture right from the start by choosing Ann Veneman as his ag secretary. The official heartwarming story line that accompanied her nomination was that she is a farm girl, raised on her daddy's

California fruit farm. The press announcement exuded the sweetness of gingham, the smell of home-baked peach pie, and images of the old home place. But the reality of her appointment was much colder and more businesslike: Veneman had made her career as a corporate lawyer, lobbyist, and faithful servant to giant agribusiness interests, particularly the DNA-splicers of the biotech industry and the global corporatizers of agriculture.

Bush's ag policy reads like it could've been written in the lobbying offices of the corporatizers, because—surprise!—it was. Bush and the people in his inner circle (as well as those in his near-outer circle) know as much about agriculture as a hog knows about Mozart. For policy direction, they naturally turned to those they know and trust, not the dirt farmers and hardscrabble ranchers of America (and damned sure not consumers and environmentalists), but the brand names of agbiz—Archer Daniels Midland, Cargill, Tyson, and others who—surprise again!—happen to be big-money backers of the prez.

Take his policy toward the heartland's amber waves of grain. Our country's incredibly efficient family farmers, blessed with rich soil and good climate, produce not just an abundance of corn, wheat, and other grains but, in most years, such a massive overabundance that our storage facilities floweth over. Farmers need a policy that allows them as a group to control their overproduction (something no individual farmer can do). By matching their production to what the world market actually needs, farmers could then get a fair price in the marketplace for their crops.

Did George, who boasts of having an MBA from Harvard, apply this basic lesson one learns in Supply & Demand 101? Of course not! He's no dummy. Well, he's no Mensa, either, but one lesson George learned early in life is: Always go with those who put the butter on your biscuits. In this case, that's the ADMs and Cargills—the giant grain traders who buy the farmers' crops and

A CORPORATE CLOD

In choosing his undersecretary for rural development, George W named a man known by his own Iowa neighbors as "the poster boy for corporate agriculture."

Thomas Dorr, head of a large corporate farming operation, says that his model for agriculture is to replace individual family farms with 200,000-acre factory farms, admitting that this makes him a "pariah" in his own community.

Dorr was named by Bush to take charge of USDA programs to help the rural poor—programs that he detests, having once complained that the "subsidy games" of rural development had turned Iowa into a "state of peasants."

Not that he detests all subsidies, since he's the willing recipient of very large crop subsidies from us taxpayers. Indeed, he so enjoys them that he has been caught twice rigging his company's books Enron-style in order to get more subsidy payments than he was entitled to receive, including one energetic grab for excess in 2002, the year Bush tapped him for his government job. Asked about his unethical conniving, Dorr shrugged, saying he had "no idea if it's legal."

Bush couldn't get the Senate to confirm this obtuse clod, so he simply slipped him into office for a year as a recess appointment. When his time was up, Dorr was then moved upstairs, where he now serves as special assistant to Ag Secretary Ann Veneman.

appreciate presidents who keep the price of those commodities low, low, low.

Bush first expressed his fealty to them on the campaign trail in 2000. Karl Rove had positioned his charge amid some hay bales on an Iowa farm, and George, dressed in farm-boy denim, uttered the word that would be, he promised, the basis for his farm policy: exports.

You could almost hear the anguished groans of family farmers and ex-farmers all across the country who'd been fed this line since the days of Earl Butz, Nixon's infamous ag secretary. Back in '73, Uncle Earl told farmers to increase their grain production drastically, to plant grain "fencerow to fencerow," to lease their neighbor's land and plant it in grain, to "get big or get out," because—trust him, he roared—we're gonna sell all that grain on the world export market!

That sounded swell, and farmers mostly went along, but what Earl and the experts weren't telling them is that every country from Brazil to Bangladesh was moving into grain exports, and that very soon there'd be a global grain glut, causing grain prices to plummet, crashing farm income, and bankrupting tens of thousands of good farmers in our country. The ones who cleaned up on this export-based policy were—guess who?—ADM, Cargill, and the other middlemen, who, like hogs loose in a cornfield, gorged themselves on practically free grain and fattened their already ample bottom lines.

So, zooming from Butz to nuts, here came George in 2000 pushing the same old line, and even promising more tax money to subsidize grain exports. These export subsidies are yet another shameful political deception. While they're hyped in the name of helping hard-hit farmers, it's not farmers who do the exporting. That's done by Bush's same ol' corporate pals, so they're the ones who pocket the subsidy funds that you and I provide.

Once in office, Bush produced a 2002 farm bill that's a whopper— a whopper in terms of its budget-busting $8-billion-a-year price tag and a whopper in terms of who it helps. Again, it was passed in the name of helping those who toil in the soil, but *60 percent* of America's farm families—especially the small farmers—get absolutely zero out of the bill, not a penny. Payouts are based on volume of production, so the giant agribusiness operations (including such corporate "farmers" as DuPont and Chevron) are the ones who get the supersized checks from us taxpayers.

The bottom line on Rancher George's "farm" program is that it aggressively squeezes good farmers out of business, bilks taxpayers who unwittingly are financing the further corporatization of our food supply, and enriches the corporatizers, who then kick back some of the profits to Bush in the form of campaign donations, hoping to keep this golden joy ride going.

NAFTA Gives the Shafta to Farmers

In 2001, at the presidential Summit of the Americas in Quebec city, our very own George W. Bush attempted to articulate his belief that all of the world's people should be grateful that he and other leaders are creating ever more supra-national trade arrangements like NAFTA and the WTO: "It's important for folks to understand that when there's more trade, there's more commerce," he explained.

Okay. Has everyone got that? More trade means more commerce. Or is it vice versa? Whatever. This is what passes for intellectual depth in the shallows of BushWorld: Trade = good. Commerce = good. More = very good.

But trade at what cost, and commerce that profits who? W doesn't address such complexities.

One way to probe the complexities of free-trade dogma is to look at the real-world results of NAFTA, hailed when it was passed in 1993 as a groundbreaking bonanza for U.S. workers, farmers, the environment, and democracy. Let's check out how our farmers have fared. Far from raising the income of our nation's farmers through a bonanza of exports to Mexico and Canada, as promised, the flow of trade has shifted dramatically. The United States now imports far more ag products than we ship out.

Prior to NAFTA, our country's ag shipments to these two neighbors were worth $200 million a year more than we bought from them. Now, we're $1.5 billion a year in the trade hole, buying that much more worth of their agricultural goods than we sell to them.

Worse, what we're importing are largely the very crops our own farmers produce—since NAFTA, 80 percent of the foodstuffs coming into the United States are products that displace the crops raised here at home. NAFTA allowed the multinational middlemen to increase production in Mexico, where they can profit from farm labor paid the subpoverty pittance of $3.60 a day, freely use pesticides banned in the U.S., and then ship those farm products back into our consumer markets without any tariffs, quotas, or effective food safety.

The official statistics of the decline of the U.S. farm-export prowess since the agreement was implemented tell an unforgiving tale that belies the rosy glow of official press releases about NAFTA's impact:

- Wheat exports to Mexico and Canada fell by 8 percent and prices dropped 28 percent.
- Corn exports fell by 11 percent and prices dropped 20 percent.
- Cotton exports fell by 28 percent, and prices dropped 38 percent.
- Soybean exports increased by 16 percent, but prices dropped by 15 percent.
- The poultry trade surplus with Mexico and Canada fell by 14 percent.
- Cattle and beef fell from a $21 million surplus to a $152 million deficit.
- The grain and cereal surplus fell by a third.

BUSH'S WTO BACKFIRE

Bizarrely, George W pushed in 2002 to get China into the World Trade Organization, asserting that this would open up this market of 1.3 billion people to food exports from our farmers.

Knock-knock. George, is *anyone* home? China is a burgeoning agricultural giant that is determined to become a powerhouse food *exporter*, not an importer. By putting them in the WTO, Bush and Congress have flung open the doors all around the world to Chinese exports, including here in the U.S.A. With their cheap labor, peasant farmers, and no environmental enforcement on pesticide rules, China's foodstuffs can swamp world markets with massive amounts of dirt-cheap farm commodities.

Take fruits and veggies—products that George W claimed our farmers could sell to China if only we let them into the WTO. In the past decade, *China has become the world's largest producer of fruits and vegetables—for example, they now grow seven times as much fruit as we do.*

Under WTO rules, the United States cannot prevent China from shipping its cheap stuff into our market, crushing the livelihoods of our fruit and veggie farmers.

- The fresh and frozen vegetables deficit more than doubled to $1 billion.
- The fresh-fruit trade deficit fell from a $9 million surplus to a $37 million deficit.
- The dairy deficit nearly doubled to $796 million.

There are similar trade declines in most other commodities, from asparagus to zinnias. With these declines, the income of U.S.

farmers has plummeted 35 percent, from $59 billion the years be-
fore NAFTA to a projected $41 billion in 2001. During the reign
of NAFTA, we've lost farms (and good farm families) at a rate six
times steeper than were lost prior to the 1993 agreement.

Well, you might think, at least our trade losses mean that Canadian and Mexican farmers have prospered, right?

Hardly. Even though Canada's food exports to the United States
and Mexico more than tripled during the NAFTA years, farmers
didn't see the gains. Indeed, farm income there fell by 17 percent
in these years, and farmers' debt zoomed up by half. The benefi-
ciaries were the processors and exporters, which are the same companies that operate here: ADM owns more than half of Canada's
wheat-milling capacity, for example, and Tyson owns 66 percent of
the beef-packing plants there.

The situation is worse in Mexico, where corn is the staple crop
and corn tortillas the staple food. NAFTA has devastated the small
corn farmers there, for it allowed the export giants to suddenly
dump millions of tons of U.S. corn (cheap, because of the price
bust for our corn farmers) into their market. The export companies now ship fifteen times more U.S. corn into Mexico each year
than they did prior to NAFTA, and these imports have cornered
25 percent of the market there, up from only 2 percent pre-
NAFTA.

At the same time, as a price for joining NAFTA, Mexico had to
alter its constitution to eliminate its historic *ejido* land-reform program that protected small farmers and guaranteed them a price
floor (like minimum wage for workers). With no price floor and a
deluge of imported corn, the price paid to Mexican farmers for
their corn has plummeted by almost half since 1993—far below
what it costs for them to produce it.

The result is that an estimated 15 million rural Mexicans have
been forced out of farming, lost their *ejidos,* and migrated to cities

or to the United States. Perversely, the price that Mexican consumers pay for corn tortillas—central to the cooking of all families and essential to the food budgets of the poor—has jumped by half.

Even more perversely, the country that identifies its cultural heritage with corn, and that had been self-sufficient in this staple, is now dependent on foreign suppliers. Whenever ADM, Cargill, and the other giant corn shippers can get a better price elsewhere, or whenever there is a corn shortage due to poor crops in the U.S. (as happened in 1996), Mexico is thrown into a food crisis.

As reported by the watchdog group Global Trade Watch: "Post-NAFTA Mexico no longer has policies to ensure it can feed itself." Welcome to the New World Order.

The Cows Have Come Home

When the first undeniable case of American mad cow disease broke into the news last December, a host of Bush officials trotted out to shout reassurances at us: "Just an isolated case" . . . "America's beef supply is the safest in the world" . . . "Trust us, we're experts." Even George told the media that he'd eaten a big serving of beef for Christmas dinner—so, see, no problem, all clean, don't think about it anymore.

Yes, admitted the Ag Department's top animal scientist, the mad cow in question was part of a herd of eighty cattle that also could be infected, but by golly, our animal-tracking system is excellent, so "we feel confident that we are going to be able to determine the whereabouts of most, if not all, of these animals within the next several days." Trust us.

Seven weeks later, the ag scientist had to admit that only one third of the suspect cattle could be found. "We never expected to be able to find all of them," he lied in classic Bushite fashion, apparently hoping we wouldn't recall his earlier promise. The other two thirds couldn't be tracked and presumably had ended up in

MAD COWS, MAD SCIENCE, AND BEAUTIFUL LIPS

Buying "beauty" is the American way—but at what price?

Take the cosmetic alterations needed to produce poufed-up lips that can give you that much-desired pouty look. What is used to produce this poufing? Cow stuff. More specifically, doctors inject lips with a gelatinous protein contained in the connective tissue of cows.

But with the mad cow scare, alarmed socialites became worried that their pouty lips could kill them. Some market-savvy doctors began assuring patients that their collagen came from "closed herds"—a sort of elite cow club that never mixes with the cow masses, particularly your low-class mad cows. One skeptical socialite wasn't buying such vague reassurances, however, and told her doctor she "wanted to visit the herd."

Luckily, thanks to the dedication of the genetic engineering industry, a non-cow alternative is now available to lip-poufing worrywarts. A bioengineered human collagen has been derived, using the foreskin of an infant boy's penis.

And science marches on.

our lunches and dinners. Declaring the investigation over, he said, "It's time to move on."

Move on? To where? To a mad cow burger? To the intensive care unit? So much for our "experts."

And when real experts do speak, the Bushites cover their ears. Ag Secretary Ann Veneman had attempted to calm public concern last December by convening a panel of international experts on mad cow disease, expecting the members to do a cursory review of the beef industry's production system, rubber-stamp the industry's mantra that America has no mad cow problem, and endorse her assertion that the government's safety rules are more than adequate to protect consumers.

But—Holy Big Mac!—the panel bolted. In remarkably direct language, Ann's panel said that mad cow disease is common in our cattle herds, that the USDA's voluntary tracking system is grossly inadequate, and that the meat industry's method of feeding rendered hogs, chickens, and other animals to cattle (which naturally are not carnivores but grass-grazing vegetarians—vegans, even) is inherently unsafe.

The experts also concluded that the reason the USDA has found only one case of mad cow disease so far is that it has not been looking very hard. Of 30 million cattle slaughtered each year, only 40,000 are tested for the deadly disease, barely one tenth of one percent. The panel chairman said that the USDA might find "a case a month" of mad cow if it was doing enough testing.

The Bushites and industry, which are always lecturing environmentalists and consumers that "science, not politics," should be the sole basis for making regulatory policy, responded to this scientific finding by playing politics. Industry lobbyists blindly reiterated the absurd claim that mad cow "poses no risk to consumers." One lobbying group, apparently auditioning for *Saturday Night Live,* complained that the scientists' report was, duh, "negative in tone" (well, yeah). This same group then invoked the Bushonian gospel, asserting that the best policy in these situations was not to get regulators involved, but "letting industry address these things."

Did I mention that meat processors and corporate cattle operators have put nearly a million bucks into Bush's presidential campaign? The Bushites can talk about "science" until the cows come home, but their policies are all about politics.

Not only do American cows have this horrific disease, but there's distressing evidence that American people do, too. Consider the Alzheimer's connection.

Alzheimer's disease, little known just a generation ago, is now so common in our land that the term has come to be used as a

WHO'S IN CHARGE?

One of the most vehement groups lobbying against tightening mad cow regulations is the National Cattleman's Beef Association. But the NCBA doesn't have to do all of its lobbying from the outside—three of its former officials now sit next to Bush's ag secretary as her top aides:

Dale Moore—secretary's chief of staff

Alisa Harrison—secretary's spokeswoman

Chuck Lambert—undersecretary for regulatory programs

joke, as in: "Excuse me for forgetting your name—I'm having an Alzheimer's moment."

Of course, it's no joke, but a cruel and fatal disease that essentially dissolves the brain, causing victims literally to lose their minds. Alzheimer's has been surging in America over the past two decades, now registered as the eighth-leading cause of death, affecting some 4 million of our people.

But there's one aspect of this that the economic and political powers in our country don't want scientists discussing in public: Autopsy studies done at Yale and elsewhere show that 20 percent of people diagnosed with Alzheimer's were misdiagnosed. They actually had another brain-wasting disease called CJD, and thousands of these cases might well be a variety of CJD caused by mad-cow infected meat that the victims had eaten years earlier.

Yes, this means that mad cow disease in humans, which the beef industry has adamantly insisted does not exist at all in America, could actually be widespread and already killing people under a pseudonym. Three minimal steps should be taken immediately to know the full truth and protect public health. First, instead of conducting mad cow tests on only a tiny fraction of the cattle slaughtered in our country each year, the USDA should test all cattle—as Japan does as a matter of course. The Bushites, however, have rejected this move—at the behest of Tyson and other big beef purveyors.

Second, the USDA should ban the feeding of any and all slaughterhouse waste to cattle. While the agency was finally forced to stop agribusiness profiteers from feeding cattle parts to their cattle (yes, cow cannibalism!), those cattle parts can still be fed to hogs, chickens, etc., which in turn can still be fed to cattle. It's secondhand cannibalism, and it can pass mad cow disease right through to your child's burger. Secretary Veneman, however, has rejected

ANTIBIOTIC INSANITY

Due largely to the overuse of antibiotics in our country, many deadly bacteria have developed immunity to penicillin and other bacteria-fighting drugs, mutating into superbugs that now threaten our public health.

Three million pounds of antibiotics are used each year to treat humans, but we're consuming much heavier doses from a surprising source: meat. Our compliant government lets the meat industry dump tons of antibiotics into their feeding troughs, not to combat disease but to cause the animals to gain weight more quickly . . . thus fattening corporate profits. As of 2001, the meat companies were feeding these staggering levels of antibiotics:

3.7 million pounds to cattle

10.3 million pounds to pigs

10.5 million pounds to poultry

BUSHSTINK

The Bushites created new rules last year to regulate the sickening stink of the massive hog factories dotting our countryside. Don't hold your breath for any improvement in the stinky-quotient, however, for Bush's rules:

• Provide that companies will have their hog factories monitored for pollution violations *on a voluntary basis.*

• Let the companies *write their own pollution-prevention plans* and keep these plans secret from the public.

• Provide that companies in violation of the antipollution rules *do not have to make any changes* in their polluting practices.

this zero-tolerance ban on cow cannibalism, not wishing to inconvenience the beef purveyors.

Third, there should be a national monitoring system of all CJD cases to determine the extent that mad cow infection is involved. This is no big deal; doctors routinely monitor and report on all sorts of other diseases so medical science can know what it's dealing with. In the past, however, when the Center for Food Safety and others formally petitioned two federal agencies for a CJD monitoring program, they were rejected. Again, let's not upset the beef purveyors.

Living High on the Hog

Where does one of the biggest hogs in the world live? Not on Old Mc-Donald's hog farm, but in a swank apartment above Park Avenue in New York City—except when he's wallowing in his other home in Aspen, Colorado.

Joseph W. Luter III is his name, and he's boss hog at Smithfield Foods, an $8-billion-a-year global giant that is the nation's biggest hog producer, as well as the biggest pork processor, accounting for more than a fifth of the pork in the USA. Luter III is also a major political player and shaper of government policies. He's on the executive committee of his industry's top lobbying group, the American Meat Institute, and his company has ponied up $650,000 for Bush and the GOP in the past four years

In his business dealings, Luter believes in controlling the pork market from "birth to bacon," and he's proceeding to do that by buying out his competitors, squeezing out the family farmers who raise hogs, and feeling free to contaminate the air and water for miles around. Of course, Mr. Joe doesn't have to breathe or drink the hog waste from his polluting factories, because—remember?— he's living in a Park Avenue high-rise and enjoying the pure mountain air of Aspen.

GOVERNMENT-SANCTIONED TERRORISM

We know about the terrorist attacks that killed some three thousand of America's people on September 11, 2001.

Few, however, know that other terrorists killed another five thousand Americans that year—and five thousand more every year since. These terrorists don't come at us in hijacked airplanes, but more stealthily in our hamburgers, hot dogs, and other meats. They are *E. coli*, salmonella, listeria, and other contaminants that are by-products of the industrialized, quick-profit meat industry. The sped-up processing lines of Tyson, ConAgra, and others routinely result in fecal contamination that produces the deadly "bacterial terrorists" that invade our bodies and kill an average of fourteen of us every day of the year, with children being especially vulnerable.

But this is a terrorist war that Bush & Company refuses to fight. Rather than forcing the meat companies to clean up their act and shutting down the killers, Bush allows voluntary self-inspection by the companies and simply sends a toothless USDA letter of reprimand to violators. So the terrorism continues unabated.

The Big Hog is unapologetic for the putrid smells and polluted waters he creates, noting simply that they're the price of progress . . . and of profits for Smithfield. Yes, he's locking up the market, but he says, "What we did in the pork industry is what Perdue and Tyson did in the poultry business." Oh, good, one bullying monopoly excuses another.

As for using his market power to crush family farmers, Luter is colder than a frozen pork chop: "The bottom line is that small farmers have been disappearing for a hundred years," he says, apparently impatient to complete the process. Meanwhile, Luter is outraged that farmers, environmentalists, and other citizens are rebelling against his hoggishness and passing state laws to rein in his greed. So he's buying pork factories in places like Poland, saying, "The current hostility from *interest groups* in this country has made other parts of the world look good to us."

If it looks so good elsewhere, Joe, may we count on your moving there with your hogs?

Frankenfood

As you're flipping through the back sections of your morning paper, do you sometimes come across a story that strikes you as the *real* news of the day? I'm talking about stories that are somewhere between reeeaaally important and jaw-dropping, and you ask yourself: Why did they bury this back here? . . . Why isn't this the front-page lead with a screaming two-inch headline?

I had one of these moments recently when I came across this deceptively bland headline: "Modified Seeds Found Amid Unmodified Crops." Most people scanning the February 24, 2004, issue of the *New York Times* either would have missed this story entirely, since it was stuck down at the bottom of page 6, section C, or would not have bothered to read beyond the boring headline, which made it seem like a farmer story.

A more appropriate headline would have been: BIOENGINEERED FRANKENFOODS CONTAMINATING U.S. FOOD SUPPLY!

Yes, it needs that exclamation point, for this is a truly alarming story that should be the subject of ongoing reporting by every media source, perhaps matching the in-depth analysis the media establishment gives to such stories of national import as, say, Michael Jackson.

[**A Little Background:** For some time, the likes of Monsanto have had their white-smocked engineers tinkering merrily and dangerously with the very DNA of food, genetically modifying the natural composition of things like potatoes so they contain a pesticide in every one of their cells, or altering rice so it contains a diarrhea drug in every bite. This is no mere lab experiment, for unbeknownst to the vast majority of Americans, Monsanto and a handful of other global biotech giants have quietly spread the seeds of these genetically altered Frankenfoods to so many farms over the past decade that about a third of the foods on U.S. supermarket shelves now contain organisms with tampered DNA—everything from baby food and milk to products made with soybean and corn. Thanks to well-placed campaign donations and powerhouse lobbying, this infiltration of our food supply has been done with practically no consumer awareness, since both Bill Clinton's and George W's administrations have let these foodstuffs be sold in America without so much as a label on them to tell us that we're buying something that our families might prefer to avoid. **We now return you to the present.**]

The industry and our so-called regulators keep saying that they have these GMOs—genetically modified organisms—under tight control so the altered plants won't spread (through their pollen or the mixing of seed) into the fields of unaltered crops. This is what you might call "important," since no one knows the long-term impact of Monsanto's lab creations on human health and on the earth's

FRANKENPIG

As anyone living around a corporate hog factory knows, hog stuff stinks. Mightily.

Should the corporations have to clean up their act and drastically cut the massive number of hogs it jams into each factory? No need, because here comes the Biotech Stink Busters!

By splicing some genes from mice and *E. coli* bacteria into pig genes, a less stinky critter has been created, which is now trademarked under the sweet name of Enviropig. It still contaminates the air and water with its excretions, but you don't notice it as much. No report on what happens to those of us who might eat ham with mice genes and *E. coli* bacteria in it.

ecology. It would be beyond stupid—biblical-level stupidity—to let this stuff escape and taint our entire food supply.

In the last few years, however, there have been unsettling "incidents": a shipment of organic corn from Texas was rejected by France (GMO foods are banned in Europe, Japan, Brazil, and other nations) because it contained the altered genes, apparently the result of pollen drifting from farms growing altered corn onto the fields of the organic farmers; a load of GMO corn not approved for human consumption ended up unannounced in Taco Bell's corn products; scientists found that monarch butterflies were sickened and dying from exposure in the Midwest to GMO grain; Mexico, which does not allow GMO corn in its borders, has found native varieties deep in the country's interior to be tainted by Monsanto's corn pollen, which had drifted hundreds of miles, much farther and much faster than the industry and our government thought possible.

Knowing this is why the small article in the *Times* caught my eye. It reported on new findings by the widely respected Union of Concerned Scientists, which had just run a series of systematic tests on thirty-six batches of corn, canola, and soybean seeds. All of the seeds were supposedly nature's own, free of any genetic manipulation. Yet UCS found that more than two thirds of the batches had traces of GMOs in their DNA.

This means that Monsanto's engineered demon is loose on the land. As one of the scientists put it, *"The door to seed contamination is wide open."*

This is our food supply we're talking about. Shouldn't this story be way up front in the papers, the lead item on the nightly news, a topic of talk-radio heat, the subject of congressional investigations, a story worthy of comment by presidential candidates? But . . . nothing. Just a small article on page C6.

Even more alarming than the findings by the scientists was the disdainful attitude of the contaminators. Did we get an "Oops, sorry about that," or an "Oh my gosh, we've gotta do something to fix this, starting with not planting any more of these seeds until we figure out the problems"? No, we did not. What we got was a demand from an industry lobbying group that other countries stop banning GMO Frankenfoods and simply learn to live with (feel the love in this statement) "acceptable levels of contamination."

A LITTLE STATE MAKES A BIG STATEMENT

While Washington is asleep at the switch, the state of Vermont is doing something. In March, by a stunning 28–0 vote, the Vermont senate passed the Farmer Protection Act to hold the biotech giants legally accountable for the contamination of any farmer's crops by a corporation's GMOs.

CLOSING THE CIRCLE

Linda Fisher spent five years as Monsanto's top Washington lobbyist. She also managed Monsanto's political money. In 2001, George W chose her to be deputy administrator of the EPA, the agency's second-highest post. The EPA has regulatory authority over plants genetically altered to contain pesticides. Monsanto is the leading producer of those altered plants.

Did I mention that it's our food supply we're talking about?

UCS was not the first group of scientists to hit the alarm button on this willy-nilly corporate splicing of assorted pesticides, bacteria, sex hormones, drugs, and animal genes into the foods we're eating. In January 2002, the National Academy of Sciences—more establishment than that you cannot get—stepped forward to say: Hold your horses, buckaroos!

In 2000, the NAS convened a panel of biologists and ag scientists to conduct a study of the process by which the Monsantos are rushing these genetically altered plants into production, into the environment, onto our grocery shelves, and into our bodies. Their study finds that there should be "significantly more transparent and rigorous" review of the testing, monitoring, and assessment of these genetic manipulations before they're unleashed on an unsuspecting and vulnerable world.

As one critic of the current regulatory system noted in welcoming the NAS findings: "It has been a cakewalk for the industry in terms of getting products approved."

It has indeed. NAS's scientific panel pointed out that the Agriculture Department presently allows corporations to plant unlimited acreages to test their experimental plants, with no independent evaluation of the danger this poses to our environment and food supply. The NAS wants this slipshod process to end, calling for independent reviews of all tests, less secrecy by the corporations, more involvement of the public before these experimental foods are approved, and long-term regulatory monitoring of any approved crops.

Science has spoken, but money shouts. Monsanto and the other food contaminators have poured more than $100 million into Washington lobbying in the past six years, and they are major campaign donors to Bush, the GOP, and the Democrats in Congress, so the essentially unregulated, let-'er-fly policy toward these dangerous organisms was written by them. The scathing NAS report was only a one-day story. If Bush even saw the report, neither he nor anyone in his administration lifted a finger to implement any of its recommendations, nor have the congressional leaders of either party.

When informed about the genetic tampering with our dinner, a good 80 percent of people polled say "Hell no!" to being Monsanto's guinea pigs. But it's the old tree-falling-in-the-forest question: "If the people shout their opposition, but Congress and the White House have Monsanto checks stuffed in their ears, do the people make a sound."

" Virtually all participants said that bioengineered foods should be labeled as such. . . . Most participants expressed great surprise that food biotechnology has become so pervasive in the U.S. food supply . . . [and] outrage that such a change in the food supply could happen without them knowing about it. "

—The "Well, duh!" findings from a series of twelve focus groups convened by the FDA, 2001

Monsanto Goes Nuts

If insanity could be packaged, Monsanto, Inc., would surely own the patent. Like a foaming-at-the-mouth mad dog, this behemoth—which has earned its nickname, Madsanto—attacks anyone who dares get in the way of its genetic profiteering.

Oakhurst Dairy in Portland, Maine, has seen Monsanto's madness in action. It's a small milk processor that tries to do business the old-fashioned way: by giving consumers what they want. Or, in this case, not giving consumers what they don't want, which is milk laced with Monsanto's artificial growth hormone, which has been linked to everything from premature puberty in children to health problems in cows injected with it.

Overwhelmingly, consumers say they don't want this stuff in their milk, so, Oakhurst Dairy started paying dairy farmers a premium for milk that's certified to be free of it. Oakhurst proudly labels its cartons with this promise: "No Artificial Growth Hormones Used."

Enter the raw nuttiness of Monsanto, the $5 billion global giant. It sued little Oakhurst, claiming that its label deceives consumers by making them think that the natural milk is healthier than milk with Monsanto's hormones. "Milk is milk!" is the cry of Monsanto, which says there's no difference between its milk and any other. But, of course, as any momma knows, there is. A big difference: Monsanto's milk has an artificial sex hormone added to it, something many moms would not choose to pour for their children.

It's not like the Oakhurst label claims its milk to be healthier. In fact, all Oakhurst is doing is letting customers know what's not in their product, so customers can make up their own minds which milk to buy. As Oakhurst's president puts it: "We're in the business of marketing milk, not Monsanto's drugs." Besides, he says, "The

A QUIZ, KIDS

How can Monsanto's artificial sex hormone additive be in your milk (without even being labeled), while every other industrialized nation in the world has banned it?

ANSWER: MARGARET MILLER

Monsanto was required to submit a report to the FDA to determine if its artificial hormones were safe. Margaret Miller, one of Monsanto's leading researchers, prepared this report. Shortly after submitting it to the agency, Margaret got another job. Can you guess where? *Bingo,* if you said FDA!

Her first job was to decide whether or not to give official approval to the report she wrote for Monsanto. Do you think she did? *Double bingo,* if you said yes!!

BONUS POINTS

Deciding whether or not Monsanto's milk containing artificial growth hormones should have to be labeled as such, so consumers know what they're getting, was a task that fell to another FDA official, Mark Taylor. He decided no, Monsanto's milk need not have a consumer label. Guess who Mark lobbied for before coming to the FDA? *Bingo-bingo-bingo,* if you said Monsanto!!!

And that, kids, is how it works.

world seems a little bit discombobulated when somebody attempts to prohibit you from doing the right thing."

Welcome to Discombobulation, USA. As Monsanto knows from experience, small businesses and farmers don't have the resources to match its legal, lobbying, PR, and political clout, so just by filing frivolous lawsuits like the Oakhurst case, it can bully its way in and get what it wants. The corporation, which had already

DO IT YOURSELF

There's a growing movement among consumers, small farmers, entre-preneurs, communities, and others to take back control of our food economy and food culture by focusing on *locally grown* foods. Farmers' markets, for example, are flourishing, with some 2,800 of them across America, involving nearly 20,000 farmers selling in all kinds of neigh-borhoods to hundreds of thousands of consumers.

There are also community garden projects, farm stands, and other direct farmer-to-consumer marketing outlets, as well as more and more grocers and restaurants proudly offering food fresh from local farms.

Buying locally means you can get better food at cheaper prices, but it also means that the money you spend stays in your community and supports a revitalized, sustainable family economy. Check it out:

www.localharvest.org

strong-armed two small dairies in other labeling cases (The Pure Milk and Ice Cream Company in Texas and Swiss Valley Farms in the Midwest), uses its deep pockets and cadre of litigious lawyers as an intimidator. Monsanto spends whatever it takes, and it was pre-pared to spend more than a quarter of a million dollars just in legal fees to force Oakhurst to change its label. How's a small dairy in Maine going to match that?

On Christmas Eve of last year, Oakhurst gave in and settled out of court, even though Maine public opinion was overwhelmingly on its side, and even though legal analysts thought Monsanto had silly putty for a case and would lose. What it couldn't get on the merits, though, it got with its money. Oakhurst's label will still say "No Artificial Growth Hormones Used," but now it will also carry a disclaimer that says: "FDA states: 'No significant difference in milk from cows treated with artificial growth hormones.'"

Yes, Monsanto has hitched the power of the U.S. government behind its onslaught, getting to use the FDA's imprimatur against small businesses, farmers, consumers, and people "doing the right thing." In case you thought maybe the government was supposed to be on the public's side, Bush's handpicked FDA watchdog for the industry, Mark McClellan, declared last year: "FDA will continue to take strong action to protect American consumers from products with labeling that is false or misleading."

Spoken like a good corporate trooper. Though Mark's sanctimonious pronouncement begs the question of what's false or misleading about "No Artificial Growth Hormones Used."

Bringing the Farm to the City

In the Brave New Biotech World of corporate agriculture, the claim is that small farmers can't compete with giant factory farms and "bio-pharms" that can produce such miracles as genetically altered crops, milk laced with artificial sex hormones, meat juiced up with steroids and antibiotics, and other wonders.

Before you swallow that bit of corporate propaganda, you might check out the Center for Urban Agriculture, located right smack in the center of suburban Santa Barbara, California. Amid the gas stations and shopping centers of this corridor of suburbia sits a small farm, the remnant of a homestead that dates back to 1895.

It's only twelve and a half acres, but Michael Ableman and his able crew produce an astonishing abundance on this fertile plot. More than a hundred kinds of fruits and vegetables spring from the land here—

> **"We'd like to keep our food un-laboratized."**
>
> **—Statement by top chefs opposed to genetically altered transgenic fish**

enough to feed five hundred families and employ more than twenty people. No genetic manipulation, no chemicals, no steroids, no lab technicians, no corporate overseers are needed to generate this cornucopia of food, which not only is efficiently produced but also bursts with flavor, nutrition, and wholesomeness that don't seem to factor into the bottom-line mentality of the Monsanto-ites.

The corporate vision of agricultural production is based on the cold concept that nature must be bent to the bottom line, and if brute force isn't working, you're probably not applying enough of it. To the contrary, Ableman and crew apply the idea that good farming is the art and science of *cooperating* with nature, rather than always trying to overwhelm it.

The center goes beyond mere food production to relating its farm to the larger spirit of community involvement, education . . . and fun—matters that the Monsantos don't give a damn about.

For another story of human gumption to cheer you, let's go to Detroit—the hard-hit, gritty city that has lost thousands of its jobs and suffered a massive outflow of population over the last few decades, leaving buildings abandoned and lots vacant. Indeed, a third of the property within the city limits is nothing but boarded-up buildings and trash-littered lots.

But today something new is growing in Detroit . . . literally. Coming off of dozens of those vacant lots are tons of hay, honey, chickens, goat's milk, tomatoes, herbs, beans, and even beef. This urban agricultural abundance is being produced by a hardy group of Detroiters who're turning Motor City into Garden City. More than forty community gardens and microfarms—working with churches, schools, food banks, homeless groups, community organizations, and activists—not only grow a cornucopia of food in the city but also process and distribute it, offering a terrific example of truly grassroots economic development.

One of these urban farmers is Paul Weertz, a science teacher who a decade ago wanted to connect his inner-city students to nature and food. He and his student volunteers have converted seven abandoned lots into ten acres of fertile farmland. Now even rabbits and pheasants have been drawn to this revitalized acreage in one of America's biggest cities—a phenomenon he calls "a totally surreal experience."

But it's real, and both economically and spiritually uplifting. Detroit city farmers are also converting an old auto shop into a community center with a greenhouse, cannery, and café, drawing other small business to the neighborhood. "Growing vegetables is just a vehicle for other kinds of change," says one farmer. These innovative Detroiters are proving that true growth comes not from corporate trickle-down but from ourselves.

High on Hemp

It was Willie Nelson who first suggested to me that hemp is "not just for breakfast anymore." And Willie is a fellow who knows quite a bit about the plant called cannabis, marijuana, pot, reefer, whatever you choose to call it.

Willie's point, however, was not to tout the smokable cannabis, but to push a strain of the plant that farmers worldwide have been raising for six thousand years to produce a cornucopia of products, including beautiful fabrics, fine paper, inexpensive fuel, safe pain relievers, and plastic substitutes.

Did you know that our Declaration of Independence was drafted on paper made of 100 percent pure-dee hemp; that *Old Ironsides* was powered by hemp-cloth sails; and that both George Washington and Thomas Jefferson cultivated the stuff? Jefferson even wrote that "hemp is of first necessity . . . to the wealth and protection of the country." And he wasn't just blowing smoke.

This isn't about "Puff the Magic Dragon," it's about an easy-to-

THE FICKLE POLITICS OF HEMP

Even though hemp had been demonized and outlawed in 1937 as part of a nutty *Reefer Madness* campaign, it got a reprieve in World War II when the military suddenly needed huge amounts of rope and other hemp products. A "Hemp for Victory" drive was launched and 400,000 acres were rushed into production. With the war's end, however, the heroic crop went back on the no-no list, where it remains today.

grow commercial crop that can produce a natural high for our economy. As for its hallucinogenic properties, industrial hemp is to marijuana what near beer is to beer—it has practically zero tetrahydrocannabinol (THC), which is the elemental oomph in marijuana that gets you high. You could smoke a pure hemp rope all day long and you wouldn't get high, you'd get sick. As an agricultural economist put it: "You'd croak from smoke before you'd get high on hemp."

Yet our ever-alert Drug Enforcement Administration classifies hemp as a "Schedule One Substance"—a no-no right up there with heroin, cocaine, and other life wreckers. Attempt to grow it and Ashcroft's drug troopers will storm onto your property, bulldoze your crop, and haul you off to the federal slammer. If he thinks you were growing hemp for "terrorist purposes," he'll send you to Guantánamo. He's nuts, but that's another story.

Suppose there was a political issue that could pull together liberals and libertarians, that could bring together the American Farm Bureau Federation and the International Paper Company with Woody Harrelson, environmentalists with small business, Democrats, Republicans, Greens, New Party members, Libertarians, Noneoftheabovers and Whatnots? Wouldn't that be worth pursuing? The legalization of hemp for America is one such commonsense grass-roots issue.

Family farmers could benefit because hemp can be a huge cash crop: It will grow anywhere in America; indeed, the damned stuff is literally a weed, growing wild in many areas.

And it has a short growing season, so it can be planted after other crops are harvested, giving farmers two incomes on the same plot of land. Plus, it's profitable. Imagine the frustration of farmers in North Dakota, who are losing money on the grain they raise, looking across the invisible border separating them from their next-door neighbors in Manitoba, Canada, where farmers are enjoying $250-an-acre profit on their hemp crop.

The environment would win, too. Commercial farming today is soaked in chemicals, causing massive contamination of the soil, water, wildlife . . . and farm families. Contrast hemp: It's natural, requiring very little water or fertilizers to produce an abundant yield, and it's naturally disease and pest resistant, so toxic chemicals are unnecessary. And its seeds can be collected to grow next year's crop.

Also, *hemp can save our forests!* It produces a top-quality pulp for papermaking and an excellent fiber that can be used in lieu of wood for homebuilding, and it's more productive than timber—for example, an acre of hemp generates more pulp than four acres of trees.

The economy also gains. As more and more of our jobs are being shipped out to Southeast Beelzebub by corporate America, hemp offers a grassroots opportunity for new economic growth and job creation. The whole plant can be used commercially—leaves, stalk, seeds, oils, and resins.

- Paper made from hemp is the best in the world—from beautiful writing papers to cardboard.
- Eat hemp! Its seeds have a wonderful flavor, great cooking versatility, and more nutrition than soybean seeds—and they're high

in essential fatty acids, vitamin E, dietary fiber. It boosts your immune system and is heart-friendly. The oil makes a great base for skin-care products.

- Make beer! Breweries in Kentucky, Maryland, and California are turning out caseloads of really good hemp brews.
- Wear it. It makes strong canvas shoes and beautiful fabrics that "breathe" naturally. Hemp shower curtains are light and—get this—do not mildew. Hemp carpets are durable and naturally flame retardant.

> **"Make the most you can of the Indian Hemp seed and sow it everywhere."**
>
> **—George Washington, 1794**

- Use it for industry. Hemp fiberboard can replace wood; its scrap can be a biomass alternative for gasoline. And it's a biodegradable substitute for plastics—BMW already uses a hemp-fiber plastic for some of its trunk and door panels, and Ford is considering it for radiator grills.

Sales of these products are around $100 million a year across America, yet our farmers can't join in the gain—all of the stalks, leaves, and seeds used to make these products have to be imported from China, England, and twenty-eight other countries where hemp is grown freely and proudly.

Bush, Ashcroft & Gang, crazed by antidrug fever, totally oppose letting our farmers—the heirs of Washington and Jefferson—raise this most useful crop. Their drug war is so stupid that if you pay close attention to just how stupid it is, it'll drive you to drugs.

How stupid is it? Ask Jean Laprise, a Canadian farmer. Birdseed is what got Laprise in trouble with America's Drug Enforcement Agency (DEA), which gives new meaning to the term *birdbrained.*

He shipped a twenty-ton load of birdseed to a U.S. customer. Some hemp seed was in the mix. The hemp seed is high in nothing but protein and is good for birds and people, but the DEA got wind of Laprise's shipment and had the whole load impounded, saying it contained a trace of the dreaded THC.

Let me give you three numbers. Marijuana must have at least 4 percent THC to get anyone high. Industrial hemp is only 1 percent THC, so you can't get high on it. Laprise's birdseed mix tested out with a THC content of 0.0014—one fourteen thousandths of a percent. Even a tiny bird couldn't get a buzz on that.

To compound this raw stupidity, the DEA demanded that Laprise recall seventeen loads of hemp-based products he had earlier shipped to the United States. This recall included hemp seed used by Nutiva, a California company that makes granola bars. As a result, Nutiva had to suspend production, forcing a layoff at the company. Also, a wholesaler, about to pick up Nutiva's bar for national distribution, backed out of the deal after it learned the DEA was messing with the company.

What the hell is the DEA smoking? It's time to free hemp in our Land of the Free.

The Mendocino Rebellion

Mendocino County has declared itself free of GMOs!

Since our happy-go-lucky corporate government in Washington has hugged Monsanto and the other GMO-makers like they're made of money—which, of course, they are—We the People have to stand up to the we-don't-give-a-damn corporations ourselves, protecting our families from their mad profit schemes.

The good folks of Mendocino County, California, took the lead last year, proposing Measure H, a ballot initiative to ban all GMO crops and animals from being raised in their county. The initiative, voted on this March, was a total community effort, supported not only by consumers and environmentalists but also by local merchants, farmers, brewpubs, wineries, and, for good measure, both the county sheriff and the public health director. It was a grassroots campaign, with both Internet organizing and old-fashioned people-to-people connections.

On the "No!" side were a consortium of state and national corporations, led by the very-green-sounding CropLife America (CLA). Yeah, green as in greenbacks. CLA is a lobbying and political front for Monsanto, DuPont, Dow, Bayer, and the other multi-billion-dollar biotech biggies. Based in Washington, D.C., these outsiders hurled half a million bucks at the Measure H proponents. That's a ton and a half of cash in a county with only 47,000 people!

But they hurled more than greenbacks, also resorting to big-city powerhouse politics. They dispatched their lawyers to try to censor the ballot language, wanting to X out certain arguments in favor of the measure, specifically demanding that voters not be told that wine made from GMO-grapes would not be allowed in European and other foreign markets. The judge ruled that the language could stay since it was a true statement. The opponents also tried to hide the out-of-state source of their funding, and they used the always unpopular tactic of negative push-polls. (These are calls to voters in which the hired callers claim to be taking an independent poll, but then ask leading propagandistic questions that trashed Measure H, such as: If you were aware that this measure was written by socialist homosexual atheists who support Osama bin Laden and have secretly worded the ballot so it will allow them to convert our schools into Al Qaeda training centers, would you be more inclined or less inclined to vote for it?)

Most comical in the election debate was the claim by the antis that regulation is a matter best left to the federal government. Sweet hypocrisy! These are corporate execs who are stomping on any Washington regulation that raises its head! If we had national regulation of GMOs, the Mendocinos would not have to be putting themselves out front. Besides, since when do people who call themselves "conservative" favor federal action over local?

When election day came, the hardy band of Measure H supporters had been outspent seven to one. But the numbers that mattered are these: They won by a lovely twelve-point margin, 56 percent to 44. As campaign sparkplug Els Cooperrider put it: "They had the money, we had the people."

Mendocino is the first, but the idea of taking a local stand against these global perverters of our food supply is spreading to other counties and states, just as it has already spread through Europe, Asia, Latin America, and elsewhere. It's a grassroots rebellion against the corporatization of food . . . and a rebellion for reclaiming our people's sovereignty over our food, economy, politics, and destiny.

BUSHFIND

Find the words listed at the bottom of the page.

```
G  R  V  H  S  S  O  J  T  S  D  O  T  T  T
C  N  R  I  G  I  A  P  P  O  L  M  S  H  Z
P  E  I  O  B  I  U  L  O  B  B  S  E  U  W
U  O  O  R  D  L  I  F  M  R  V  U  V  P  H
R  L  X  Y  E  C  N  E  C  O  F  L  R  M  J
B  M  P  A  I  E  S  N  O  E  N  L  A  E  A
A  Z  I  N  K  Z  N  K  X  I  W  E  H  H  Q
N  X  G  N  S  B  J  I  D  U  K  N  L  I  S
A  O  A  V  L  O  U  Y  G  V  F  K  A  L  P
G  R  U  A  E  Y  A  X  E  N  J  P  C  D  A
F  S  E  N  O  M  R  O  H  R  E  S  O  N  C
A  N  T  I  B  I  O  T  I  C  S  O  L  Q  F
R  I  S  O  M  G  V  H  A  H  F  K  I  A  M
C  A  R  G  I  L  L  E  E  Z  M  I  R  B  O
B  K  U  E  J  N  H  R  N  O  S  M  P  E  N
C  Y  H  M  T  V  U  J  R  E  E  U  C  I  S
O  M  K  K  C  S  L  J  B  R  M  E  F  H  A
B  G  A  E  A  E  Y  H  S  C  G  A  J  R  N
P  C  O  E  A  I  Z  L  J  E  B  E  N  N  T
R  I  M  R  N  K  Z  H  F  D  T  L  M  C  O
```

ANTIBIOTICS	BIOENGINEERING	CARGILL
DORR	FARMERS	FOOD
FRANKENFOOD	GMOS	HEMP
HORMONES	LOCAL HARVEST	LYSTERIA
MEASURE H	MONSANTO	OAKHURST
SALMONELLA	SPLICING	VENEMAN

Solution on page 226.

You'll Never Have to Feel Alone Again, My Friend

☞ *Homeland Security, USA Patriot Act (I and II), FBI, CIA, DEA, ATF, INS, DARPA, ARDA, TIA, CTS, PAL, CAPPS II—and so much more is now out there for us, created or greatly expanded by George to keep us safe.*

*S*ecurity. Need I say more?

As a child, didn't you get the warmest, most comforting feeling inside you from knowing that your momma and daddy were watching over you day and night? Of course you did. And you can thank your lucky stars that today you've got an equally concerned Watch Daddy in the Oval Office. Bush cares so much about you—about all of us—that in only four years he's spread a big, poofy security comforter over every city, neighborhood, village, and hamlet in America. Each and every one of us is now covered 24/7, 365 (and also on that 366th day we get every Leap Year).

George has his trusted team headed by John Ashcroft, Don Rumsfeld, Tom Ridge, Bob Mueller, George Tenet, and so many *others (think of them as his helpful elves, fairies, leprechauns, sprites, and munchkins!) keeping watch over us at work, in our homes, through our computers, in our churches, at our banks, on the streets, in our libraries, at our political gatherings, and, well, everywhere. He and his concerned team have devised all sorts of neat new laws, rules, programs, secret panels, and technologies to know, at any given moment, where everyone is, what we're doing, and whether we're being bad or good.*

Unfortunately, as in every big family, there are some bratty malcontents and misfits out there who are not properly grateful for the president's prudent program of surveillance. They keep prattling on about their precious little rights, as if it's their individual freedom that matters. These selfish ones fall down kicking and screaming about their "freedoms" every time Bush makes another bold move to tighten up the Homeland, doing what he has to do to secure America's freedoms.

So what if Ashcroft wants to see your health-care records or check out your bank account—what've you got to hide, sister? So what if the army or HSD Counterterrorism Units infiltrate your discussion groups—what are you discussing that you and your ilk don't want the authorities to hear?

And the worst, the ones that make me wanna puke at the sorry sight of them, are the lefty, Dixie Chicks–loving, ACLU-type squirrels who constantly go around waving the Bill of Rights (which, I remind you, was not part of the original Constitution) and shrieking about their freedom to "dissent." Dissent? We're in a war against all the world's evildoers, you Benedict Arnolds, so sit down and shut up—or go live with Osama bin Laden, that's what I say. My commander in chief, George W, got it right when he told us: "There ought to be limits to freedom."

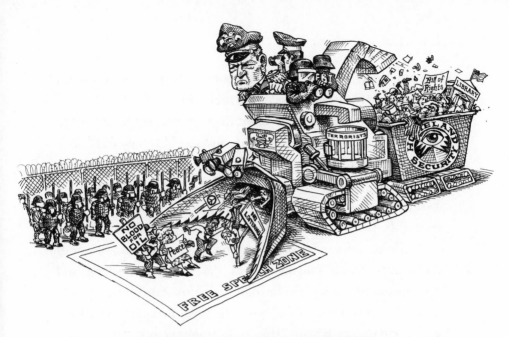

GEORGE W DOES LIBERTY

The musician David Baerwald is not a household name to most Americans, but in the richly creative world of singer-songwriters, he's a standout. Particularly appealing to me is that he doesn't shy away from focusing on the political realities of the day. In the mid-nineties he produced an album titled *Triage,* and for the liner notes, he offered this dedication to forty years' worth of America's nefarious governmental spooks and liberty-busters who had led our democracy so deeply into the shadows of autocracy: "This record is dedicated to Dean Acheson, Paul Nitze, John J. McCloy, John Foster Dulles, Allen Dulles, Henry Kissinger, James Baker III, and George Bush in the sincere hope that there is a God and that he is vengeful beyond all comprehension."

Imagine what David might write about today's list of liberty-busters and privacy-invaders who are so aggressive, so intrusive, so arrogant, so insatiable, so obtuse in their reach for ever-greater executive power over the American people that they make the above lineup seem almost prissy. Indeed, some on Baerwald's list would be shocked and amazed (if not appalled) that not only the Bushites but also battalions of private corporate intruders have moved America so deeply and quickly into the darkness.

One issue that powerfully binds the right and left in our country is their shared distrust, suspicion, and (dare I say it?) *HATRED* (yes, Hightower, you do dare!) of those who carelessly trim—much less whack at, bludgeon, and negate—our Bill of Rights for their own political and economic gain. After all, 228 years ago, the assault by British Redcoats on individual privacy and their trampling of the Colonists' freedom of expression and association was one of the most passionate rallying cries for the American rebellion, and that passion breathes yet in the bosom of most Americans.

In Washington and on Wall Street, however, that passion has been squashed flatter than roadkill by the shortsighted rush of the elites to gain more money and power for themselves. Democrats in Congress have offered only lame lip service to protecting our liberties, fearful that a White House hell-bent on amassing more executive and police authority will tar them as soft on Osama. Meanwhile, both parties willfully pave the way for still more privacy invasions by corporations, which happen to finance their campaigns.

The intruders, whether governmental or corporate, always insist that their every incremental incursion on our rights is done solely for our own good: "We must balance your freedom with concern for your security," they coo to us. "We need to collect all of your financial, health, and other records in our databases in order to offer you better service and more convenience," they assure us, ever so soothingly.

Never in our nation's history has the rude grab for our First, Fourth, and Fifth Amendment rights been so sweeping. Let me give you just one glimpse of it: the Bushites' heavy-handed lockdown on our essential right of protest, crude assault that, curiously, the media establishment has either avoided covering or quietly applauded.

BushCheneyAshcroftRumsfeld&TheBoys cannot just come out

and ban protest, of course, but they can intimidate and marginalize it . . . and they are doing exactly that with total abandon. We observers in Texas are not at all surprised by George W's full support for suppressing protest, for he used his governorship as a time to practice his chops.

What we have at work here is the fundamental problem of former CEOs controlling the executive branch of government, for CEO-world is one of toe-the-line, don't-rock-the-boat, don't-challenge-authority deference to number one. Corporations are essentially hierarchical autocracies, the very opposite of democracies, which have a way of being messy, noisy, disorderly, and ofttimes raucously disobedient.

> **" There are more instances of abridgement of the freedom of the people by gradual and silent encroachments of those in power than by violent and sudden usurpation. "**
>
> —*James Madison*

The Bushites, as the world has now learned, are barkers who intend to do it their way, so don't bother them with any democratic niceties or test their patience with your unauthorized opinion. Bush himself not only recoils from dissent but is also determinedly dismissive of both dissenters and their right to dissent.

As governor back in 1999, he and his clever staff devised the Bush Doctrine of Contained Dissent as a way to keep pesky protestors away and to keep him in a serene political bubble. What they did was literally corral protestors into distant protest pens (how delightfully cowboyish this must have seemed to George, who'd recently acquired his Crawford ranchette and was really getting into his Western Man persona. Yippie-ty-yi-yo!).

Their first move was against a small group of Texans, mostly senior citizens, who were protesting some of Bush's most atrocious environmental policies. They were carrying colorful signs and peacefully walking up and down the public sidewalk in front of the governor's mansion, not disturbing anyone. This sidewalk has historically been the site of Texas protest, and while previous governors undoubtedly wished that the balky citizenry of their time would go away, none tried to act on their wish.

But in '99, George was gearing up for his presidential run, and scads of national-media types were coming in from out of town to evaluate this politically hot governor. Having protestors draw attention to his record of servitude to corporate polluters was definitely off message, so Bush unleashed his state police detail to swoop down on the picketers and order them removed to a faraway parking lot, which they arbitrarily designated as a "protest zone." It was conveniently beyond the sight and sound of His Gubernatorial Eminence . . . and of the media. Those protestors who objected to this sweep were promptly arrested, cuffed, and thrown in jail.

As you might expect, such thuggishness was completely illegal, and a judge later threw the state's trumped-up charges out of court, reopening the public sidewalk to (O, democracy!) the public. But by the time this decision came down, George and Karl were long gone, safely in the White House.

BushZones Go National

At the 2000 GOP nominating convention in Philadelphia, candidate Bush created a fenced-in, out-of-sight protest zone that could hold only a few hundred people at a time. So citizens who wished to give voice to their many grievances with the Powers That Be had to:

- Schedule their exercise of First Amendment rights with the decidedly unsympathetic authorities.
- Report like cattle to the protest pen at their designated time, and only in the numbers authorized.
- Then, under the recorded surveillance of the authorities, feel free to let loose with all the speech they could utter within their

allotted minutes. (Although no one—not Bush, not convention delegates, not the preening members of Congress, not the limousine-gliding corporate sponsors, and *certainly not* the mass media would be anywhere nearby to hear a single word of what they had to say.)

Imagine how proud the founders would be of this interpretation of their Revolutionary work. The Democrats, always willing to learn useful tricks from the opposition, created their own Free Speech Zone when they gathered in Los Angeles that year for their convention.

Once ensconced in the White House, the Bushites institutionalized the art of dissing dissent, routinely dispatching the Secret Service to order local police to set up FSZs to quarantine protestors wherever he goes. The embedded media trooping dutifully behind him almost never cover this fascinating and truly newsworthy phenomenon, instead focusing almost entirely on spoon-fed sound bites from the president's press office.

An independent libertarian writer, however, James Bovard, chronicled George's splendid isolation from citizen protest in last December's issue of the *American Conservative* (www.amconmag. com). He wrote about Bill Neel, a retired steelworker who dared to raise his humble head at a 2002 Labor Day picnic in Pittsburgh, where Bush had gone to be photographed with worker-type people. Bill definitely did not fit the message of the day, for this sixty-five-year-old was sporting a sign that said:

> *The Bush Family*
> *must surely love the*
> *poor, they made so*
> *many of us.*

Ouch! Negative! Not acceptable! Must go!

Bill was standing in a crowd of pro-Bush people who were gathered along the street where Bush's motorcade would pass. The Bush backers had all sorts of "Hooray George" type of signs. Those were totally okeydokey with the Secret Service, but Neel's . . . well, it simply had to be removed.

He was told by the Pittsburgh cops to depart to the designated FSZ, a ballpark encased in a chain-link fence a third of a mile from Bush's (and the media's) path. Bill, that rambunctious rebel, refused to budge. So they arrested him for disorderly conduct, dispatched him to the luxury of a Pittsburgh jail, and confiscated his offending sign.

At Bill's trial, a Pittsburgh detective testified that the Secret Service had instructed local police to confine "people that were making a statement pretty much against the president and his views." The state judge not only tossed out the silly charges against Neel but scolded the prosecution: "I believe this is America. Whatever happened to 'I don't agree with you, but I'll defend to the death your right to say it'?"

This was no isolated incident. Bovard also takes us to St. Louis, where George appeared in January 2003. About 150 sign-toting protestors were shunted off to a zone where they could not be seen from the street, and—get ready to spin in your grave, Jimmy Madison—the media were *not allowed* to talk to them, and protestors were *not allowed* out of the protest zone to talk to the media.

Now meet Brett Bursey. He committed the crime of holding up a "No War for Oil" sign when sensitive George visited Columbia, South Carolina, last year. Standing amid a sea of pro-Bush signs in a public area, Bursey was commanded by local police to remove himself forthwith to the FSZ a half-mile away from the action, even though he was already two football fields from where Bush was to speak. No, said Brett. So, naturally, they arrested him.

Asked why, the officer said, "It's the content of your sign that's the problem."

Five months later, Brett's trespassing charge was tossed on the rather obvious grounds that—yoo-hoo!—there's no such thing as a member of the public trespassing on PUBLIC property at a public event. But John Ashcroft is oblivious to the obvious, so the Justice Department of the United States of America (represented in this case by—can you stand it?—U.S. Attorney Strom Thurmond Jr.) inserted itself into this local misdemeanor case, charging our man Brett with a *federal* violation of "entering a restricted area around the president." Great Goofy in the Sky—he was two hundred yards away, surrounded by cheering Bushcalytes who were also in the "restricted area."

As I write this, Bursey is still being persecuted by Ashcroft, Thurmond, and Bush. Bursey's lawyers asked for the Secret Service documents that set forth their official policies on who gets stopped for criticizing the president, where, when, and why. Ashcroft is trying to block his access to such policies, if they exist at all.

Then there's the "Crawford Contretemps." In May of 2003, a

> **"These individuals . . . may walk out into the motorcycle route and be injured. And that is really the reason why we set these [protest zones] up, so we can make sure that they have the right to free speech, but, two we want to be sure that they are able to go home at the end of the evening and not be injured in any way."**
>
> —*Secret Service agent Brian Marr, explaining that corralling people in protest zones is really for their own good*

troupe of about a hundred antiwar Texans were on their way by car to George W's Little Ponderosa, located about five miles outside of the tiny town of Crawford. To get to Bush's place, one drives through the town, but the traveling protestors were greeted by a police block-ade. They got out of their cars to find out what was up, only to be told by Police Chief Donnie Tidmore that they were violating a town ordinance requiring a permit to protest within the city limits.

But wait, they said, we're on our way to Bush's ranchette; we have no intention of protesting here. Logic was a stranger that day in Crawford, however, and Chief Tidmore warned them that they had three minutes to turn around and go back whence they came, or else they'd be considered a demonstration, and, he reminded them, they had no permit for that. (Tidmore later said that he actually gave them seven minutes to depart, in order to be "as fair as possible.")

Five of the group tried to talk sense with Tidmore, but that was not possible. Their reward for even trying was to be arrested for re-fusing to disperse and given a night in the nearby McClennon County jail. The chief said he could've just given them a ticket, but he judged that arresting them was the only way to get them to move, claiming they were causing a danger because of the traffic.

This February, the five were brought to trial in Crawford. Their lawyer asked Tidmore if someone who simply wore a political but-ton reading "Peace" could be found in violation of Crawford's or-dinance against protesting without a permit. Yes, said the chief, "That could be a sign of demonstration."

The five were convicted.

The Bushites are using federal, state, and local police to conduct an undeclared war against dissent, literally incarcerating Ameri-cans who publicly express their disagreements with him and his policies. The ACLU and others have now sued Bush's Secret Ser-vice for its ongoing pattern of oppressing legitimate, made-in-America protest, citing cases in Arizona, California, Connecticut,

Michigan, New Jersey, New Mexico, Texas—and coming soon to a theater near you!

If incarceration is not enough to deter dissenters, how about some old-fashioned goon squad tactics like infiltration and intimidation of protestors? In May 2002, Ashcroft issued a decree terminating a quarter-century-old policy that bans FBI agents from spying on Americans in their political meetings and churches.

Not only were federal agents "freed" by Bush and his attack dog Ashcroft to violate the freedoms (assembly, speech, privacy) of any and all citizens, but they were *encouraged* to do so. This unleashing of the FBI was done in the name of combating foreign terrorists. The Bushites loudly scoffed at complaints that agents would also be used to spy on American citizens for political purposes having nothing to do with terrorism. While officials scoffed publicly, however, an internal FBI newsletter quietly encouraged agents to increase surveillance of antiwar groups, saying that there were "plenty of reasons" for doing so, "chief of which it will enhance the paranoia endemic in such circles and will further service to get the point across that there is an FBI agent behind every mailbox."

> **"To those who scare peace-loving people with phantoms of lost liberty . . . your tactics only aid terrorists."**
>
> **—John Ashcroft**

Likewise, in May of 2003, the Homeland Security Department waded butt-deep into the murky waters of political suppression, issuing a terrorist advisory to local law enforcement agencies. It urged all police officials to keep a hawk-eyed watch on any home-landers who [**Warning:** Do not read the rest of this sentence if it will shock you to learn that there are people like this in your country!] have "expressed dislike of attitudes and decisions of the U.S. government."

MEMO TO TOM RIDGE, SECRETARY OF HSD: Sir, that's everyone.

All 280 million of us, minus George Bush, you, and the handful of others actually making the decisions. You've just branded every red-blooded American a terrorist. Maybe you should stick to playing with your color codes.

Last November, Ashcroft weighed back in with new federal guidelines allowing the FBI to make what amounted to preemptive spying assaults on people. Much like the nifty Bush-Rumsfeld doctrine of attacking countries to preempt the possibility that maybe, someday, some way those countries might pose a threat to the United States, the Bush-Ashcroft doctrine allows government gumshoes to spy on citizens and noncitizens alike without any indication that the spied-upon people are doing anything illegal. The executive directive gives the FBI authority to collect "information on individuals, groups, and organizations of *possible investigative interest.*"

The language used by Ashcroft mouthpiece Mark Corallo to explain this directive is meant to be reassuring, but it is Orwell-level scary: What it means, says Corallo, is that agents "can do more research" . . . "It emphasizes early intervention" . . . "allows them to be more proactive." Yeah, they get to do all of that without opening a formal investigation (which sets limits on the snooping), much less bothering to get any court approval for their snooping. A proactive secret police is rarely a positive for people.

With the FBI on the loose, other police powers now feel free to join in the all-season sport of intimidating people. In Austin, even the army was caught snooping on us. At a small University of Texas conference in February to discuss women's issues in Muslim countries, two army officers were discovered to be posing as participants. The next day, two agents from the Army Intelligence and Security Command appeared on campus demanding a list of participants and trying to grill Sahar Aziz, the conference organizer. Alarmed by these intimidating tactics, Aziz got the help of a lawyer, and the local newspaper ran a story. The army quickly went away, but a spokeswoman for the intelligence command refused even to confirm that the agents had been on campus, much less discuss why the U.S. Army is involved in domestic surveillance and intimidation.

In California, an antiwar group called Peace Fresno included in its ranks a nice young man named Aaron Stokes, who was always willing to be helpful. Unfortunately, Aaron died in a motorcycle wreck, and when his picture ran in the paper, Peace Fresno learned that he was really Aaron Kilner, a detective with the sheriff's department. The sheriff said he could not discuss specifics of Kilner's infiltration role, but that there was no formal investigation of Peace Fresno under way. He did insist, however, that there is potential for terrorism in Fresno County. "We believe there is," the sheriff said ominously (and vaguely). "I'm not going to get into it."

If the authorities think there is terrorist potential in Fresno (probably not real high on Osama's target list), then there is potential everywhere, and under the Bush regime, this is plenty enough reason for any and all police agencies to launch secret campaigns to infiltrate, investigate, and intimidate any and all people and groups with politics that they find even mildly suspicious . . . or distasteful.

**"*I've heard of such a thing, but not since the early 1950s, the McCarthy era.*

"*It sends a troubling message about government officials' attitudes toward basic civil liberties.*"

—*Georgetown University law professor David Cole on John Ashcroft's subpoenas in February trying to get private information about participants in an antiwar forum at Drake University, Des Moines, Iowa*

The attitude of police authorities was summed up by Mike Van Winkle, a spokesperson for the California Anti-Terrorism Information Center (another spinoff of the Homeland Security Department—your tax dollars at work). After peaceful antiwar protestors in Oakland were gassed and shot by agents of the Anti-Terrorism Task Force, Van Winkle [**Note:** I do not make up these names] explained the prevailing thinking of America's new, vast network of antiterrorist forces:

You can make an easy kind of link that, if you have a protest group protesting a war where the cause that's being fought against is international terrorism, you might have terrorism at that protest. You can almost argue that a protest against that is a terrorist act. I've heard terrorism described as anything that is violent or has an economic impact. Terrorism isn't just bombs going off and killing people.

The Miami Model

Last November, George W crossed the Atlantic to powwow with First Pal Tony Blair. Fearing mass protests against the Bush-Blair misadventures in Iraq, White House political operatives demanded that London police ban all protest marches and shut down the central city for three days, creating an exclusion zone to keep George from having to see or hear any protests.

Having done that, George then had the temerity, chutzpah, and audacious hypocrisy to refer to England's antiwar protestors in his featured speech, saying with a smug smile and patronizing tone: *"'I've noticed that the tradition of free speech—exercised with enthusiasm—is alive and well here in London. We have that at home, too.'"*

Ironically, on the same day that Bush was cynically posturing in England as Mr. First Amendment, I was in Miami, experiencing first-hand some of that free speech tradition he said we have "at home."

I was there for the citizen protests against the Free Trade Area of the Americas. This trade scam is NAFTA on steroids, not only allowing corporations to extend their job busting, farm-bankrupting, environment-contaminating, sovereignty-destroying practices to more than thirty countries in this hemisphere, but it also would open up all of our public services to corporate privatizers—from postal service to water, from social security to health care.

Trade ministers from thirty-four nations were gathering at the Inter-Continental Hotel in Miami to seal the FTAA deal, meeting behind closed doors with only corporate executives and lobbyists allowed to take part in the negotiations. Since We the People were being shut out by the insiders, about ten thousand of us decided to show up outside the hotel where the elites were secluded. From labor unions to students against sweatshops, from Baptists to Quakers, from farmers to environmentalists, we were there as a well-organized and determinedly peaceful protest.

We had an approved location for our big gatherings, we had permits for our various marches, we had prenegotiated agreements with the police, we had our own AFL-CIO Peace Keepers trained to deal with rowdies—in short, we were playing it by the book. We were also playing by the biggest political book of all—the Constitution and Bill of Rights.

But we quickly learned that, for this week at least, Miami was not America. We were shocked to find that, as Leo Gerard, president of the United Steelworkers put it, "a massive police state was created" to intimidate us, deny us our most cherished rights—and attack us again and again. The Powers That Be, obviously fearful of people actually trying to practice democracy, amassed an unprecedented force armed to the teeth and commanded to treat law-abiding citizens as the enemy.

Forty different police agencies—federal, state, county, and city—deployed more than 2,500 heavily armed troops against us

in about a two-square-mile section of downtown. Phalanxes of police stormed down the streets in full combat uniforms, with most
of the police covered head to toe in all-black riot gear, eyes hidden
behind Plexiglas face shields. Intersection after intersection was
blocked by a solid wall of fifty to a hundred of these troops, all
wielding three-foot truncheons, high-voltage stun guns, concus-
sion bombs, rifles loaded with skin-piercing hard rubber bullets,
tear-gas guns, blinding pepper spray, and other weaponry.

They were everywhere—on rooftops peering through binocu-
lars, in surveillance boats along the bayfront, in vans and cars that
rushed in screeching convoys from place to place, in helicopters
that constantly chopped the air above us. At the amphitheater,
where I emceed Wednesday night's People's Gala and spoke Thursday morning to a rally of retirees, the presence was overwhelming . . .
and menacing. Everyone had to pass through a gauntlet of fifty or
so armed and scowling troops to enter the place (which was completely enclosed by a chain-link fence), and there was a brand-new,
ready-for-action, military attack vehicle parked ominously just
outside the amphitheater's entrance, complete with a black-clad
trooper standing atop it in a "Terminator" pose.

The authorities had been planning this assault for months. A
number of absurd (and unconstitutional) ordinances were rammed

WHERE DID THE MONEY COME FROM?

Remember that $87 billion that Bush got Congress to pony up last year for his
military occupation of Iraq and Afghanistan? In the budget request for this
money, *$8.5 million of it was surreptitiously allocated not for
use abroad, but for the armed force that was to be assembled to
confront us American protestors at the FTAA meeting in Miami.*

through the city council, including requiring a permit for any gathering of more than six people for longer than twenty-nine minutes and prohibiting the use of wood stilts (all passed at the last minute so they would not be overturned in court before the protest was over). Also, fire trucks were readied for use as water cannons by Miami police chief John Timoney, who is notoriously thuggish toward citizen protestors, calling them "punks," "knuckle-heads," and assorted four-letter epithets.

Union leaders, in particular, were astonished by the rampaging abuse they experienced and saw at the hands of Timoney's troops. These men and women tend to be flag-waving, police-respecting patriots who've spent their lives playing by the rules—and they felt totally betrayed by the Ashcroftonian America they saw in Miami. In a terse, one-page memo entitled "Police Repression," the AFL-CIO noted that it had "negotiated for months with local police so that our members' Constitutional rights to peaceful protest would be respected, [but] the police broke nearly every promise."

It began with senseless harassment. The retiree rally, for example, started late and had a sparse crowd, because Timoney's troops broke an agreement to let twenty-five busloads of seniors be dropped off at the amphitheater.

More than half of the buses were not allowed to enter the area at all, meaning that hundreds of totally unthreatening old folks (many of them war veterans and some of whom had traveled more than a thousand miles) were unceremoniously stripped of their First Amendment rights of assembly and free speech. Most of the other buses were stopped well short of the event—an act of auto-cratic disrespect that forced seventy-, eighty-, and ninety- year-olds to walk up to two miles to an approved event, most of which they missed. One of the retiree leaders, a proud Miami resident, ad-dressed Timoney and the mayor through a press conference: "You had the opportunity to make our beautiful city a shining star in the eyes of the country, and instead your department looks like a bunch of storm troopers."

Then came the storm. Among the experiences itemized in the AFL-CIO memo were police "advancing on groups of peaceful protestors without provocation and deploying tear gas, pepper spray, and rubber bullets on these protestors without a warning to disperse or provision of a safe route" . . . "arresting retirees, union members, and other peaceful protestors on false charges and with unnecessary violence" . . . "mistreating those arrested."

Here are just a few of the stories of people caught up in what became known as "Miami Vise:"

- Bently Killmon, a seventy-one-year-old retired airline pilot from Fort Myers, told the *Miami Herald* that he and other members of the Alliance for Retired Americans were trying to get to their buses late Thursday. "We ran into a line of brown shirts [the uniforms of Dade County police]. They were very rude. They would not let us pass and they sent us down the railroad tracks. That's when we saw the black shirts coming at us [the uniforms of Miami police]. They were pointing their guns at us. I was just incredibly frightened. Everyone in our group was knocked to the ground and handcuffed. I had my hands cuffed behind my back for 7½ hours. I still don't know what it was I did." After he spent the night in jail, the trumped-up charges against him were dismissed by a judge.

- Rubber bullets were whizzing at 120 miles an hour. A reporter for commondreams.org told of an assault by police marching in a long column at several hundred protestors, firing indiscriminately at the crowd: "One woman had part of her ear blown off. Another was shot in the forehead. I got shot twice, once in the back." A columnist for the *St. Petersburg Times* reported that a young woman was shot three times, including taking a bullet in the butt at point-blank range when she stooped to pick up a bandana she dropped. The officer had kicked her bandana away before shooting her. A friend was shot seven times trying to help her up. The woman was then shot in the back while trying to leave the area.

- The wife of a retired steelworker from Utah complained to police who were roughing up some students at the entrance to Friday's AFL-CIO rally. She was slammed to the ground facedown and police put a gun to back of her head. Her entire body was literally vibrating with fear, and she had to be taken to the hospital for the wounds she suffered. In another steelworker encounter, a union secretary and a union parade marshal wearing a bright orange vest clearly marked "AFL-CIO Peace Keeper" were returning to their hotel. Armed police commanded them to abandon the sidewalk and proceed down some trolley tracks. When they did, they were immediately pounced upon, handcuffed, and taken to jail.

- John Heckenlively, a reporter with indymedia.org, got caught in the crosscurrents of chaos during a pepper spray, tear gas, and rubber bullet assault on protestors in midtown. Trying to leave the area, he and six others came face-to-face with a cordon of

> **"Pretty disgraceful, what I saw with my own eyes. And I have always supported the police during my entire career. This was a real eye-opener. A disgrace for the community. [I saw] no less than twenty felonies committed by police officers. I probably would have been arrested myself, if it had not been for a police officer who recognized me."**
>
> **—Judge Richard Margolius, presiding over cases against FTAA protestors, December 11, 2003**

hundreds of police that filled an entire block from edge to edge. An officer told them to get out, and John replied that that's exactly what they were trying to do. Instantly, they were all arrested and John spent more than four days in jail. He was charged with disorderly conduct; his arrest form had the wrong time and place of his brief encounter with the police and falsely said that he "became violent and had to be placed under arrest." John says that "Many others in our group had similar fairy tales on their booking sheets. We think the Miami Police Department should be in the running for the Pulitzer Prize in creative fiction."

• You didn't even have to be a protestor to get caught in the vise. There was the lemonade guy, for example—a young Minnesota firefighter who was on vacation and pulled off the interstate for a lemonade. Coming out of the store, he was greeted by a huge covey of cops. He asked which direction to go to get out of their way, and when he tried to do as he was told, they arrested him. He was treated to a free twenty-four-hour stay in the Miami jail. Likewise, a Miami couple casually went out for a visit to a friend's apartment. The lobby of the building was filled with police, who told them to leave. They did—and were promptly arrested. In jail, the guy asked his cellmates to explain the FTAA to him, saying: "If I'm going to be arrested for something, I at least want to know what it's about."

There were a few widely televised instances of anarchist-looking rowdies skirmishing with the riot police, but the skirmishers turned out to be the police! Tom Hayden, reporting on the FTAA for AlterNet.org, tells of one bloody encounter apparently sparked by a couple of protestors. Then he saw the "protestors" metamorphose: "I watched through a nearby hotel window as two undercover officers disguised as 'anarchists,' thinking they were invisible, hugged each other. They excitedly pulled Tasers and other weapons out of their camouflage pants, and slipped away in an unmarked police van." There were many similar reports (including photographs printed by the Independent Media Center at ftaaimc.org) of supposed radicals in ski masks and black clothing standing, laughing, and marching with Timoney's forces—and, in some cases, gleefully joining the police in attacking and illegally arresting protestors.

Where was the establishment media? Why did they not cover this astonishing paramilitary assault for what it was? Because they largely went undercover, too, willingly abandoning any pretense of journalistic objectivity and gullibly swallowing the establishment-concocted claptrap that Miami was under siege by havoc-wreaking protestors. Rather than cover the FTAA issue or the truly interesting phenomenon of a broad coalition of citizens standing up to the FTAA's power grab, both national and local media focused breathlessly on the spoon-fed details of police preparation and combat-style movements to "defend" against the invading hordes.

What I personally witnessed in Miami, versus the news reports I saw and read, were two different worlds. The coverage was so superficial and unskeptical that it was embarrassingly silly, not only

---

OH, THANK YOU, YOUR SUPREMENESS!

In 2003, right-wing Supreme Court Justice *Antonin Scalia* declared that he sees no constitutional problem with federal authorities taking away individual rights during Bush's war:

"The Constitution just sets minimums. Most of the rights that you enjoy go way beyond what the Constitution requires. [In wartime] the protections will be ratcheted right down to the constitutional minimum. I won't let it go beyond the constitutional minimum."

missing the story but devolving into rank propaganda. Hayden caught a typical instance of the media's attitude when the local ABC affiliate ran a clip of a young woman, her fingers aloft in a V-sign, was shot at point-blank range: "The local ABC commentator said without the slightest evidence, 'She took a rubber bullet in the stomach, she must have done something. You wanna play, you gotta pay.'"

The media literally went undercover—not with the citizens who were facing the power establishment, but with the establishment's troops. Just like in Iraq, dozens of so-called journalists allowed themselves to be "embedded" within (as in "get in bed with") police.

Lest you think that this was a Miami aberration and nothing that'll affect you, this abhorrent, un-American strategy of intimidating and assaulting anyone who actually dares to use their rights in a mass demonstration against the establishment's elitist policies was done with the participation of the Justice Department and the White House, using funds authorized by Congress. Miami mayor Manny Diaz exulted that what happened there was "a model for Homeland defense," and many cities sent law enforcement observers to study what is now called "The Miami Model."

Bush Rewrites the Founders

Mixed emotions are what a doctor feels when he notices that his wife has started eating an apple a day.

These days, true conservatives are having mixed emotions about George W, who keeps strengthening the power of the federal police by weakening our right to individual privacy. The latest expansion of Big Brotherism by this so-called conservative president is a new law embedded in the 2004 Intelligence Authorization Act. It got no publicity, for Bush quietly signed it on the same day that Saddam Hussein was captured.

SHHH, THE PRESIDENT IS THINKING

In 2001, George W was asked what the Fourth of July meant to him:

" It means what these words say, for starters. The great inalienable rights of our country. We're blessed with such values in America. And I— it's— I'm a proud man to be the nation based upon such wonderful values. "

George seems to brush off irony like it's lint. While he was crowing that Iraqis were now "free," he was further restricting our freedoms with this new provision. It allows the FBI to rummage through a broad array of our personal records without having to show a judge any evidence or even a suspicion of criminal activity on our part. All the FBI has to do is file a "national security letter" asserting that you or I are "relevant" to one of its many security investigations.

The FBI already had been given the autocratic power to snoop through our bank records, but Bush's new law says the feds can secretly ransack the records held by our stockbrokers, car dealers, travel agencies, phone companies, lawyers, Internet providers, pawnbrokers, casinos, post offices, and other places. It amounts to the reincarnation of the hated "general search warrants" that the British used against the Colonists.

Oh, posh and tosh, retort the Bushites, this is only for suspected terrorists, so you have nothing to fear . . . unless, of course, you're a terrorist. There's the rub. Under their infamous USA Patriot Act, "terrorist" has been so broadly defined that it includes practically anyone they (or future governments) want to go after.

Bush pushed his new Big Brother law through a committee that met in secrecy, without bothering to hear any concerns from the public. A guy who calls himself a conservative didn't deem it worthy to consult the people as he cavalierly rewrote the Fourth Amendment genius of Madison. One Bush backer in Congress dismissed any concern by saying: "This was really just a technical change."

Holy George Orwell! When they say that expanding federal police power is just "technical," grab your Bill of Rights and run.

Et Tu, Postmaster?

The U.S. Postal Service's official logo proudly features a sharp-eyed American eagle. Most Americans, however, would be shocked and amazed to learn that we are the ones getting the eagle eye from the post office.

This is another sorry case of police power running amuck, now intruding so deeply into our privacy that federal authorities are compelling even well-meaning postal clerks to be surveillance snitches on their own customers. These authorities say they want to combat money laundering. Fine. Not so fine, however, is that they are targeting innocent citizens who buy money orders or make other money transactions at our post offices.

Through a special surveillance program called "Under the Eagle's Eye," clerks are being trained to watch for "suspicious activity" and to file a report on such customers. What qualifies as "suspicious"? *Insight* magazine obtained postal service training materials that instruct clerks thusly: "The rule of thumb is if it seems suspicious to you, then it is suspicious." Did someone buy $2,500 worth of money orders three days in a row? Suspicious. Did someone buy $25,000 worth of credit for their office postage meter? Suspicious.

These are most likely to be perfectly legitimate transactions, but clerks are told they must assume criminality, fill out a suspicious activity form, and report the customer. Forget "innocent until proven guilty"—a postal clerk's report on you can be zipped to the

Financial Crimes Enforcement Network and be distributed to police agencies worldwide without your even being informed. In the training materials, clerks are told that "It's better to report ten legal transactions than to let one illegal transaction get by."

New Toys for Big Brother

It's back. The Thing That Just Won't Die has returned in mutated form to terrorize the good people of our country, gorging itself on gargantuan fistfuls of our First and Fourth Amendment rights.

The Thing was once known as TIA—Total Information Awareness—the Orwellian/Frankensteinian creation of John Poindexter, the disgraced, convicted, and totally loopy former operative from the Reagan White House. Brought in from the cold by George W, Poindexter set up shop in a wing of the Pentagon called DARPA—Defense Advanced Research Projects Agency.

At DARPA, the maniacal Poindexter put together his TIA, a supercomputerized program to gather every scrap of data there is on everybody—from our bank accounts to video rentals, our medical histories to photos of protests we've attended. All of this was to be sifted and sorted, ostensibly to detect suspicious behavior that would tag someone as a possible terrorist.

Noting that this would make millions of Americans suspected terrorists and amount to a wholesale invasion of our people's privacy, the public screamed, Congress cut off TIA's funding, and Poindexter ultimately was forced back to Disgraceland.

But, wait . . . TIA didn't die. It metamorphosed from DARPA to ARDA—Advanced Research and Development Activity. While publicly pretending to kill TIA, congressional leaders had quietly funneled money to ARDA to resurrect TIA as The Thing, which is now pursuing the exact same assault on our privacy as TIA was, even using some of Poindexter's old crew.

ARDA says that its Thing can wolf down a "petabyte or more"

of data. How much is that? A petabyte will hold forty pages of text on every man, woman, and child in the world, with room left over to get information on your dog and parakeet.

Meanwhile, don't feel sorry that poor DARPA had its TIA stripped from its hands, for the defense agency has gotten its hands on another fun new toy. It's CTS—Combat Zones That See. This is an urban surveillance system that uses thousands of cameras linked to a central computer to track, record, and analyze the movements of every vehicle in a city. Its software can identify your car by size, color, shape, license plate . . . and even by your face. It lets authorities—either governmental or corporate—keep an unblinking eye over everyone's movements in entire cities. CTS can "track everything that moves," storing and catagorizing this phenomenal amount of data so that it is instantly retrievable. Act suspicious . . . and CTS flashes an alert to authorities, complete with your profile.

Don't worry, says DARPA, CTS is only for foreign surveillance. But that's news to the corporate contractors developing CTS. "The whole theme here is homeland security," says one bluntly. Once the technology is developed, there'll soon be versions for sale to everyone from shopping centers to private detectives.

Our Loopy Attorney General

Can we all admit, whatever our political persuasion, that America's present attorney general is at the very least . . . strange? I'm talking about strange to the point of loopy.

Forget that he was such a political extremist in his one U.S. Senate term that he was defeated by a dead man; forget that he's such a religious extremist that he periodically has himself anointed in "holy oil"; and forget that he's such a moral extremist that he had the Justice Department's famous "Spirit of Justice" statue covered because lady justice was depicted with a bare breast.

It's his crackpot, autocratic assaults on our liberties that suggest to me that he has slipped from strange to sicko. Let's review a few of his greatest hits:

- In November of 2001, while the entire federal government was supposedly riveted on that little terrorism problem we had, Ashcroft unleashed federal agents to run door-busting, commando-style dawn raids on state-approved medical marijuana facilities in California. These places treat horribly ill and terminal patients, using doctor-prescribed doses of marijuana to relieve their chronic nausea and terrible pain—all approved by the state's voters in a 1996 ballot initiative. But John, an antimarijuana absolutist, asserted his personal beliefs (as well as jackbooted federal power) to trump state policy and bust sick people, seizing patient records and the clinic's supply of the medical plants.

- A month later, our tinhorn autocrat rushed into Oregon to overturn the state's right-to-die law, again asserting personal ideology and federal power to overturn the people's will. The Oregon law, passed by a popular referendum, allows patients with less than six months to live to get a lethal prescription so they can end their suffering and die with dignity. No way, bellowed John (who seems to have a thing about forcing people to endure deathbed suffering). He issued an edict that any doctor prescribing the legal, life-ending dosage would have their license to prescribe drugs stripped by his office.

- Last year, he went after federal prosecutors, demanding that all U.S. attorneys get in lockstep with his extremist, hidebound views on crime. First he ordered prosecutors to seek the death penalty in every case where it's authorized by a law, even when the local authorities think a case doesn't warrant it. Then he commanded prosecutors to bring most severest charges possible in every criminal case and to cease using plea bargains as a tool to achieve justice. Ignoring reality, Ashcroft's imperious order removes discretion from on-the-ground prosecutors, further centralizes power in the Washington bureaucracy, and imposes a one-size-fits-all prosecutorial straitjacket that will inevitably produce injustice.

• This year, Mad Dog John's extremist views on abortion have led him to use the awesome power of his office to go after hospitals in four cities, attempting to commandeer the private medical histories of women who have had abortions in the last three years. What about patient privacy? Kiss it good-bye, says Ashcroft. In arguments for this case, he declares that "there is no federal common law" to protect patient-doctor privilege, and then, in an autocratic declaration of breathtaking arrogance: *"Individuals no longer possess a reasonable expectation that their [medical] histories will remain completely confidential."* Yes, John just tried to erase the Fourth Amendment.

> **" The Justice Department is always looking for better ways to protect the American people. "**
>
> **—Bush spokesman Scott McClellan**

How goofy is our AG? Ask the folks out in Humboldt County, California. At 6:00 A.M. on February 24, 2003, three local citizens who own glassblowing companies had their homes stormed by federal agents. The three were arrested as part of Ashcroft's nation-wide sweep, dubbed (and I'm NOT making this up): Operation Pipe Dreams.

It seems that these legitimate and well-established businesses, which employ quite a few glassblowers, were making all sorts of glass products, including glass pipes. These pipes can be used (and I know you'll see the horror of this) for inhaling what the federal agents called "controlled substances"—specifically marijuana. So the three were charged with conspiracy to sell "drug paraphernalia."

In announcing that nearly three dozen of these glassblowing fiends had been nabbed nationwide on that same day, Ashcroft warned in a voice right out of the old *Reefer Madness* movie that "the illegal drug paraphernalia industry has exploded."

Lucky for you and me, though, our nation's top cop is unleashing the full force and might of the USofA to stop glass-pipe blowing. Standing side by side with Ashcroft, the head of the Drug Enforcement Agency also piped up with this keen insight: "People selling drug paraphernalia are in essence no different than drug dealers."

You'll be pleased to know that this imminent threat to our national security has been made such a priority that Operation Pipe Dreams includes the combined forces of the DEA, U.S. Marshal, Secret Service, customs agents, Postal Inspection Service, and of course, the office of General Ashcroft.

Shredding Ashcroft

Let's hear it for America's librarians! The old stereotype of librarians being meek maidens whose only passion is for the Dewey decimal system has never been true, but now that image is being shattered for good, replaced by a new image of librarians as feisty fighters for freedom.

Who has rushed to the barricades of our nation's democracy, daring to confront John "Mad Dog" Ashcroft as he rips into our Bill of Rights and tries to strip We the People of our hard-won personal liberties? Not Congress—it's meekly going along, providing the authority and funding for Ashcroft's maniacal assault. Not the puffheads of the media—they're too busy shouting "patriotism" and cheering the Bushites to see, hear, or speak any evil by the emperor.

Instead, our gutsy defenders of liberty are librarians in cities and towns throughout the country. They are distributing information and joining public discussion groups to tell us about the freedom-busting legislation that Ashcroft cynically titled the USA Patriot Act. This thing is a Little Shop of Totalitarian Horrors, including provisions in Section 215 that compel librarians to turn over to the FBI the reading, research, and Internet records of any and all library users, prohibiting librarians from even telling you that your records have been seized by government agents.

To battle back, librarians are doing everything from issuing public warnings to refusing to cooperate. Many have also added a new piece of essential machinery to cope with Ashcroft's Brave New America: the paper shredder. Rather than hold your records, librarians are now routinely destroying as many as possible so they don't have to be complicit in Ashcroft's destruction of our Fourth Amendment right to privacy.

Their efforts have been so effective that Big Bad John had to come off of his throne and try to shut them up. His tactic was to assert that all their worrying was worthless, for his agency used Section 215 power over our library records exactly *zero* times.

Take that, you carping civil-liberty softies! Ashcroft gloated that he hoped librarians would henceforth cease spreading any more "hysteria."

But the gleam of John's gloat faded when the obvious follow-up question was asked: If this invasive authority has been deemed useless by those pursuing September 11 terrorists, why should it stay on the books? It was truly hysterical to hear Ashcroft's PR flack respond lamely that . . . well . . . uh . . . while we haven't busted any library patrons so far . . . we might feel the need do so any day now.

Exactly.

Oh, says Ashcroft, don't worry, because we're using this Patriot Act only to chase terrorists, so you can trust us not to go after *your* library records. Hello! If the founders thought we could trust authority, they wouldn't have bothered with the Bill of Rights.

The Patriot Act does not limit use of its liberty-busting police powers to terrorists, and his PR flack has since admitted that the feds are already using the act's numerous provisions for "garden variety" investigations of Americans who have nothing to do with terrorism.

Spy, Inc.

What's a spook to do? The cold war is over, the Ruskies are now our buddies, the Butchers of Beijing have become our business partners . . . so where's a spy to go to get a job?

Try Motorola, it might be hiring. The *Wall Street Journal* reports that Motorola has a substantial spy shop, with "units sprinkled in almost all of their outposts around the world." Indeed, it seems that just about every major U.S. corporation now employs spooks to go into the global cold and spy on their competitors, on foreign governments, and . . . well, who knows who else they're spying on? Actually, the term *spying* is too déclassé for the pin-striped corporate crowd. "Competitive intelligence" is the preferred designation, or, as one corporate snoop calls his espionage activities, "specialized management consulting."

This is not some rogue basement operation either. It goes right to the top of the company. The *Journal* notes that Motorola's clandestine network, created and headed by a former CIA operative, is central to executive suite decisions, with the spooks sitting in on most corporate strategy sessions. "The concept was to mirror the interaction between the CIA and the White House," says the agent who set up Motorola's shop.

There are enough of these corporate 007s that they've even established their own trade association, with nearly seven thousand members. The corporate spies use all sorts of sophisticated new software to do their espionage, but there's plenty of old-fashioned spy stuff, too—from paying informants to rummaging through a competitor's trash. Even the CIA winces at some of the practices of the private-sector spooks—as one agent put it: "In corporate America, the definition of what's ethical is what's legal."

And, as we learned from Enron, WorldCom, and the rest, they've always got corporate lawyers to help them define legal as whatever needs to be done.

The Intrusion Industry

If you've worried that Big Brother is watching you, check over your other shoulder; Big Daddy is watching you, too.

Corporations—from banks to HMOs, drug chains to credit-card giants—are poking into our private records, snooping on us as we work, following us in the marketplace, tailing our Internet movements and otherwise matching government agencies in their disdain for our right to be left alone and to keep our personal matters to ourselves.

With its campaign donations and armies of lobbyists, this burgeoning intrusion industry has not only fended off most efforts to stop them but has been able to get new laws and rules to pry open more of our private lives for their profit-seeking purposes.

For example, do you know where you are?

Not the physical you—you're right there. But the little "digital you" that banks, credit-card firms, insurance companies, brokerage houses, and other financial corporations have created from personal information that they've gleaned from you—information you thought was private. For example, how much liquor have you charged to your credit card, what's your net worth, have you missed a loan payment, are you taking medicine for a sexual problem, what's your monthly take-home, did you make a series of one-night trips to Las Vegas last year?

All this and more is collected by your financial institutions and, thanks to a little-known law that Congress passed five years ago, those institutions can now share all of your personal data, compile it into a detailed profile, and store this digital you inside their computers. But they don't stop there. The Gramm-Leach-Bliley Act lets them give "you" to all of their conglomerate affiliates and to sell "you" to other corporations under joint marketing agreements. The digital you is their slave . . . and the actual you doesn't know which corporations have you or what they're doing with you.

You can thank former Texas senator Phil Gramm for this theft of your privacy. At the behest of the industry (which, coincidentally, just happened to be his major campaign funder), Phil, who chaired the Senate banking committee at the time, dutifully maneuvered this body-snatching bill into law. Gramm left the Senate in 2002 and was rewarded with—what else?—a fat-cat job with USA Warburg, a giant financial firm that had lobbied for this bill.

BOSSES WHO SPY

A study done by the American Management Association of nine hundred of its member corporations finds that *two thirds* of them record their employees' voice mail, e-mail, or phone calls, rummage through their employees' computer files, or videotape their employees. About a fourth of the companies that spy on their employees don't even tell them they are being watched.

Worse, most of this is legal. The publisher of *Privacy Journal* reports that, under current law, "Employees are generally at the mercy of employers. There is no protection in the workplace."

Corporate Cancellation of the Sixth Amendment

In 2002, I got a note from the swell folks at Fleet, which was then my credit-card company. Actually, not a note, but a "Notice":

"This Notice is to advise you that the following Arbitration Provision will be added to your Cardholder Agreement," it cheerfully began. Hmmm, I thought, arbitration. What needs arbitrating? So I squinted at the tiny print they used in this little four-page notice, which had no eye-catching graphics, no whimsical colors, and none of the chatty style you find in other bill stuffers that the companies really want you to . . . well, notice. Indeed, it's as though Fleet didn't truly want me to notice this Notice.

But, I thought, don't be cynical, so I plunged into the prose: "This Arbitration Provision will apply to all claims." Claims? Like what? Down in the fine print Fleet told me. Sort of: "The term 'claim' means any claim, dispute, or controversy between you and us arising from or related to this agreement, any prior agreement that you may have had with us or another credit card issuer from whom we acquired your credit card account or the relationships resulting from the agreement of any prior agreement, including . . ." yada yada yada.

Whoa, I said aloud, trying to uncross my eyes, what's the bottom line here? Then I found it. Fleet's notice practically shouted that if I filed any kind of claim against it for fraud, false advertising, invasion of privacy, or whatever, it could deny me "the right to litigate that claim in court or have a jury trial on that claim." Instead, I'd have to go to an arbitration firm of Fleet's choosing, and "The arbitrator's decision will be final," even though "rights that you would have had if you went to court may . . . not be available in arbitration" and "the fees charged by the administration may be higher than the fees charged by a court."

What I had in my hand was a legalized corporate sneak attack on our Sixth Amendment right to a trial by jury.

Bye-Bye, Medical Privacy

Have you been to a pharmacy lately? If so, you've probably been handed a brochure with a form for you to sign, indicating that you have received notice of how the pharmacy deals with your private medical information.

At the top, these notices are reassuring, proclaiming something like, "We'll guard your privacy like a screeching momma eagle protecting her baby eaglets." But, alas, these "privacy policies" don't stop there, and instead go on for several pages filled with small, dense type—as though they really don't want you to read it, much less understand it.

The only reason pharmacies are suddenly expressing concern about our privacy is that a new law requires them to give written notice of their policies. I recently got one issued by the national drug chain Walgreen's, whose official corporate slogan is "The Pharmacy America Trusts." Hmmm. If they have to tell us they're trustworthy, are they?

At the top of their eight-page notice of privacy practices, Walgreen's flatly declares: "We will not use or disclose your [personal health information] without your written authorization . . ." But then comes this kicker: *"except as described or otherwise permitted by this notice."* Uh-oh, here we go. The brochure then lists twenty-two ways in which they can peddle our medical privacy.

It turns out that Walgreen's will turn records loose anytime requested to do so by workers' comp authorities, local police, an opposing lawyer in a court case, the Secret Service, the Pentagon, the FBI, the CIA and other federal intelligence agents, the homeland security czar, and a category called "other." Also, they can use our medical records "as part of a fundraising effort."

But, says Walgreen's, we customers do have the right to "request restrictions" on how they use our information. But it's only a request—"We are not required to agree to those restrictions," reads the corporate document.

Catch-22, the Corporate Version

Burton Caine, a professor of constitutional law at Temple University, went to Sprint to get cell-phone service. OK, said the clerk, give me your social security number. Say what?! Why the hell does Sprint need my social security number? It's company policy to get customers' numbers as IDs, was the reply. No, said Caine.

He knows his rights. If you still have your actual social security card, you'll note that it says plainly: "Not to be used for Identification." But Congress never passed enforcing legislation. So retailers, banks, employers, driver's license agencies, and all sorts of other corporate and governmental entities now routinely demand your personal number—it has become our de facto national ID, the Constitution be damned.

> **❝You have no privacy, get over it. ❞**
>
> **—Scott McNealy, CEO of Sun Microsystems, Inc.**

Professor Caine, however, just said no. OK, said Sprint, but to get cell-phone service, you'll have to give us your passport number and pay a $120 deposit. Then, something truly 1984ish happened. Sprint informed a credit agency that his credit was no good, and the agency put out a bad report on Caine's financial worthiness, despite his having a sterling credit rating up until the Sprint incident.

In letters to the credit agency, he demanded to see his record. Guess what the agency said? We can't give you a copy of your record unless you tell us your social security number!

Letting Consumerism Get Under Your Skin

Have you been "chipped" yet?

A company called Applied Digital Solutions wants you to undergo a surgical procedure to implant a tiny RFID microchip in your arm. Why would you want to do this? Because Radio Frequency ID chips will eliminate the heavy burden of having to carry credit cards and remember your ATM numbers. Instead, your arm *becomes* your card and ID number; simply run your arm under a scanner and your embedded radio chip sends a digital signal to the computer, allowing you to complete your transaction. ADS calls its microchip VeriPay.

There's only one rational reason that ADS executives think we'll submit to this: They're insane.

Insane but serious. They insist that this technological leap is needed because many people lose their credit cards. "VeriPay solves that problem," says a corporate PR flak, cheerfully noting that ADS's chip "is subdermal and very difficult to lose. You don't leave it sitting in the backseat of a taxi," he said.

Subdermal or not, your ID number can still be stolen by a geeky thief who rigs up a device to intercept your radio-transmitted number, then plays it back later to your ATM machine, emptying your account.

If your number is stolen, or if you simply switch credit-card companies or banks, what are you to do? No problem, says the PR guy: "If you don't want it anymore . . . you can go to a doctor and have it removed. I call it an opt-out feature," he said gaily. Swell, instead of simply calling your credit-card company to cancel your card, you'd have to call a surgeon. This is progress?

By the way, the honchos of ADS are such business geniuses that the company's stock plummeted from $12 a share three years ago to about forty cents today. I wouldn't entrust two bits to them, much less my arm.

Okay, say corporate technologists, if not your arm, how about your finger?

McDonald's, Thriftway, Kroger, and other retailers now offer "finger scanning." They put your index finger on an image reader that digitally records thirteen unique points about your finger and stores the encrypted information in the central computers of a data management corporation. Henceforth, you don't need a credit card to pay—just run your own personal finger under the scanner, and the central database records your purchases and deducts money from your bank accounts or charges it to your credit card.

Oh, yes, there is that. In addition to your finger biometrics, you do have to turn over your personal account numbers to the faraway database corporation, which gets a transaction fee every time they ring up a purchase on your digit. But don't worry about your privacy, says a Thriftway executive, because the system is "foolproof." Oh, yeah? Tell that to the teenagers who seem to have no trouble hacking into the top-secret database of the U.S. Pentagon.

But it's convenient, says the man from Thriftway. It takes only about a minute to input your index finger into the system. One short minute, and it's in there *forever*—you'll never get it back. But this selling of your privacy biometric is a small price to pay for not having to worry anymore that your credit card might be lost or stolen, say those pushing this latest technological marvel. Hello! Criminals are clever. Instead of mugging you for a credit card, now they can just chop off your finger and go on a shopping spree!

If some corporation asks for your index finger, I suggest giving them your middle digit instead.

BUSHSCRAMBLE

Unscramble the scrambled words.

1. HATSFROC _ _ _ _ _ _ _ _

2. PICYVRA _ _ _ _ _ _ _

3. OREGWEG _ _ _ _ _ _ _

4. ARNECHETT _ _ _ _ _ _ _ _ _

5. SMANIOD _ _ _ _ _ _ _

6. EREF CHSEEP _ _ _ _ _ _ _ _ _ _

7. ICLVI IEESIBLTR

   _ _ _ _ _ _ _ _ _ _ _ _ _ _

8. TIECRSUY ELMOAHDN

   _ _ _ _ _ _ _ _ _ _ _ _ _ _ _ _

9. WOELRL _ _ _ _ _ _

10. OPARTINEO PPEI SADMRE

    _ _ _ _ _ _ _ _ _ _ _ _ _ _ _ _ _ _ _

Answers on page 227.

Rugged Individualism, Compadre

☞ *By whacking budgets, privatizing government, and eliminating public services, George W is freeing our people to return America to its glory days when great fortunes could be built on that golden ethic of "let the strongest survive."*

It's all about building what George likes to call the Opportunity Society. And, as we've seen, he jumped on this job like a gator on a poodle. Didn't he have the boldness right from the start to take $3 trillion tax out of the government vaults and put them smack in private hands? You bet your snakeskin boots he did. And that $3 trillion will provide a heap of opportunity for those deserving people.

Even when the nitpicking nabobs of negativism squawked that this money was needed to provide health care and stuff like that—and when they got even squawkier about Bush giving nearly all of the money to the richest people—George hung in there like the fountainhead of corporate virtue he is.

155

He knows that what America needs right now is tough love. This society has gone squishy soft by expecting to get public schools, public parks, public libraries, public roads, public garbage pickups, public art museums, public golf courses, etcetera ad nauseam. George saw this softness, and he also saw that even more squishiness was coming, for so many people are out there crying about the "need" for public health care for everyone. He knew he had to act fast to protect Americans from their own weakness for public services—so he simply removed the money. Genius!

As for giving the bulk of the money to the top 10 percent or even the top 1 percent, let me ask you this, pilgrim: Why shouldn't the doers in our society be rewarded? After all, it's the queen bee that keeps the hive buzzing, isn't it?

It's true that, in the 2000 election, when Bush referred to his tax-cut plans he said, "Those in the greatest need should receive the greatest help." *But people misconstrued his meaning. He didn't say "the needy," as in poor people. No, he logically intended for the "greatest need" to refer to those at the top who need to get the money because they have the capacity to maximize its return for their families. Those of us who know him thought his statement was perfectly clear and consistent with his lifelong philosophy.*

If you're going to build an opportunistic society you've gotta go with those who see their chances and grab them—something George W knows from personal experience. These achievers are the ones who build businesses like Harken Energy Company and Halliburton, and it's only a matter of good policy and simple fairness that they would get the lion's share of the president's help. Let's be clear: It's the 10 percent in our country who "do." The other 90 percent are "wishers"—and we damned sure can't count on wishers to keep America the #1 Boss Hog in the world, now can we?

But you can count on the bleeding-heart, jelly-spined liberals to keep having attacks of knee-jerkitis, trying to pander to all those millions who are clamoring pitifully for help in hard times. Hard times? Have you checked the Dow Jones, sport? You want help? Get a job! Wal-Mart's always hiring.

George W is your perfect model for how you should act. Did he ever ask for public assistance to make ends meet? Hell no! He fended for himself—he got into Yale, joined the national guard, got into the oil business, swung a sweet deal for a piece of a baseball team, became a multimillionaire, went into politics to serve his nation and . . . well, there he is. Didn't you ever hear of bootstraps?

You liberals, however, don't respect such self-reliant upward mobility. Instead of celebrating the achievements of the rich and successful, they want to hobble the strong, heroic, free-market achievers among us. They worry about what happens to the Holy Everybody, tossing around code phrases like "the common good" and "lend a helping hand." Silver-tongued socialism, that's all that is. And I warn you, it's the kind of soft thinking that'll send our great country down the dangerous path toward egalitarianism.

Not for me. I'll take rugged, get-it-for-yourself individualism, offered by a guy who knows how to run government like a business.

GEORGE W DOES THE COMMON GOOD

Observing from afar, it seems to me that "Being Bush" must be such a great joy. *Reality* never seems to intrude, his own *lies* (including whoppers) seem sincerely to be believed by him, *irony* never strikes his noggin, *hypocrisy* seems to be a welcome old friend, *doubt* never darkens the door of his absolute certainty, and he thinks *introspection* means taking your car in for a checkup.

Very few presidents in our nation's string of forty-three have been as brazenly servile to the moneyed elite as has George (only Grant, McKinley, and Harding are even competitive). And none have been so blithely obtuse to that servility, couching every single act as being for "the children," "the single mom," "the small farmer," "the seniors," or some other humble group that actually gets none of the action.

He reminds me of the fable from which we get the term *naked truth*. It's about two goddesses, one named Truth and the other named Falsehood, who went skinny-dipping. When Falsehood came out of the water, she put on Truth's clothes and left. When Truth came out, however, she refused to put on Falsehood's clothing, preferring to go home naked.

George sees no virtue in naked Truth when Falsehood's garb is so readily available and such a natural fit, and he reaches for it regularly to cloak his steady undermining of the common good. One quick example: the Patient's Bill of Rights. Remember this issue? It was hot in the 2000 election, as people were outraged by the abuses they receive from their HMOs and insurance companies.

Bush grabbed this people's issue and ran with it, loudly touting his record as Texas governor, including this TV ad on his behalf: "While Washington deadlocked, he delivered a patient's bill of rights that's a model for America." Good stuff. Only it was totally false. A patient's rights bill did pass, but he *vetoed* it at the behest of a major campaign funder who owned the biggest HMO in the country, Colombia/HCA. Then, against his active opposition, the Texas legislature passed another version, this time by a veto-proof margin. Even then, George refused to sign it, letting it become law without benefit of his gubernatorial imprimatur.

Yet throughout the 2000 election he claimed to be Mr. ConsumerMan, promising to fight like an enraged bear for a national patient's bill of rights: "It's time for our nation to come together and do what's right *for the people*."

Where did Papa Bear go? Four years later, We the People still don't have that bill of rights. Bush made no fight for it—in fact, he no longer bothers mentioning it. The issue didn't go away; polls today show that four out of five Americans continue to want such a law. Bush simply lied, feigning interest in the common good as a cloak to get elected, bide his time, let the media move on to other issues . . . and let his HMO and insurance backers escape scot-free from any public accountability for their abuses.

The Bushites are laissez-faire purists striving for their ideal of a corporate-run state. Not only does this mean removing public restrictions on corporate power, it also means removing anything and everything that has the word *public* attached to it—from education to social security, housing to health care, national forests to our local water supplies. Their extremist antigovernment agenda, culled from a sprawling cluster of right-wing corporate-funded think tanks, is so sweeping and is being pursued so energetically that one can imagine them holding predawn pep rallies each day in the White House and every government agency, complete with pom-poms and cheerleaders:

> *New Deal, bad deal!*
> *Push it back, push it back,*
> *Waaaaaaaaaaay back!*

Hey, hey, what do you say?
Let's defund government today!

Privatize! Cannibalize!
Minimalize! Trivialize!
Downsize! Vaporize!

Georgie, Georgie,
He's the Man!
If he can't do it,
No one can!

It's our "commons" that they're out to eliminate. The commons is both the common wealth that all of us own together, plus the public institutions that we've established for our common good. The common wealth includes such physical assets as our air, airwaves, pure water, the ozone layer, and all of nature, as well as such intangible assets as human rights and liberties. The public institutions of the commons run the gamut from our national treasury to schools, water systems, wildlife preserves, elections, postal service, and parks.

Bush & Company are not merely trying to take us back to the Gilded Age of pre–New Deal, robber-baron corporatism, but also all the way back to the "enclosure movement" of eighteenth-century England. Back then, with the blessing of Parliament, the dukes and barons of the aristocracy suddenly laid claim to the forests, meadows, wild game, and other resources that, up till then, all had shared (and the peasantry had literally relied on for sustenance), enclosing this commons as the private property of the elites.

Three centuries later, here we go again, for Bush has blessed a gold rush by today's corporate elites to privatize our commons, while also denigrating, defunding, and eliminating our public institutions. As usual, George couches every step down this path as the very opposite of what he's doing. For example, he says we must strengthen and even "save" social security as a public retirement program. How's he proposing to do that? By converting it to a *private* program, beginning now with individual retirement accounts run by and for the likes of Citigroup, Goldman Sachs, and J.P. Morgan Chase–Bank One—all of which were caught up in the corporate scandals of the past few years. We're supposed to count on them?

Or look at Bush's signature domestic program: education. *"Leave no child behind!"* he cried, and then deliberately underfunded or axed the budgets of core education programs, while constantly highlighting public school failures, attacking teachers' unions ("terrorist" organizations, as his education secretary called them), and pushing hard for vouchers to destroy the very concept of public education, turning our children over to corporate and religious instruction. Yet donning the clothes of Falsehood, he's still campaigning as "the education president."

> *"You teach a child to read, and he or her will be able to pass a literacy test."*
> —George W

Everyone from politicos to CEOs to editorialists pound the pulpit with the same mantra: Education is absolutely key to individual and national success, the very ticket to upward mobility, and the wellspring of renewal for America's democracy. Yet for all their talk, these leaders are failing our children abysmally by letting the capacity of public education decline. Instead of doing what every honest analyst says has to be done—investing more public money to produce smaller size classes, to retain good teachers, to repair America's dilapidated school infrastructure, and to make sure every child has the preschooling and resources needed so he or she arrives ready to learn—our so-called leaders resort to quick-fix gimmicks.

The latest and most glaring is George's No Child Left Behind Act, based on the simple notion that everything will be superswell if only public schools are held accountable for their success or failure in educating kids. Sure, performance evaluation is good—who opposes that? The glitch, however, is in the gimmick. Accountability, as every parent and teacher has learned to their horror, will now be determined by a standardized, one-size-fits-all series of tests given to children as young as the third grade.

Fail the test, and not only does the child pay a price, but so does the school and the entire school district, including having their funding slashed. The pressure on all—third graders, parents, teachers, principals, superintendents—is so intense that the real-life effect of Bush's CEO-style accountability is that the education of our kids is being abandoned in favor of "teaching to the test." The schools drill the test questions and answers into each child day after day, hoping that most of them memorize enough to pass so Bush won't yank the school's funding. Never mind whether students *really* learn (as in learning *how* to learn and developing their cognitive ability). Under No Child, everything they need to know is on the test, isn't it? It's what you might call the narrow view of knowledge.

PRIORITIES

In 2003, Bush offered the Turkish government more money in a bribe to get them to send troops to Iraq than he provided for American schools to help them implement his No Child Left Behind Act.

Besides being a pitifully inadequate measure of educational progress, Bush's testing scheme is being forced on public schools without the funding necessary to administer it. This underfunding is the result of—what else?—another Bush lie. He got Congress

PLAYING GAMES WITH PUBLIC SCHOOL FUNDING

Just blocks from the U.S. Capitol, the PTA of Capitol Hill Cluster School held another fund-raiser in February. The PTA of this middle-class school has raised more than $100,000 during this school year. Is the money going to provide special school trips, treats for kids, or other educational extras?

No, the parents are having to hold bake sales and such to buy things like paper, paint, ink cartridges, locker parts, and hardware—the chewing-gum-and-baling-wire basics to fix the children's wobbly chairs, make structural repairs to the buildings, and provide essential school supplies. AP education writer Ben Feller reports that this money scramble by PTAs is now common, for public schools all across our country have seen their classroom budgets slashed so deeply by irresponsible politicians that there's not enough to cover teacher salaries, sports equipment, art supplies, and other basics that make schools run.

It's also common that teachers, themselves poorly paid profession-als doing perhaps the most important job in America, have to dig into their own thin wallets to buy books, chalk, visual aids, and other classroom essentials for the children.

The same politicians who shortchange teachers and kids are the ones who then cynically accuse the public schools of failing, and who demand vouchers from taxpayers to privatize American education.

(and specifically Senator Ted Kennedy) to pass his NCLB on the solemn pledge that he would back the law with an agreed-upon level of federal dollars.

Yet in this year's budget, after asserting rhetorically that it fulfills his promise of "making sure our children get educated," Bush shortchanges his own landmark education initiative by $9.4 billion. That's *billion!* This is on top of the $17 billion he'd cut from the No Child Act in the previous two years. This is why states from Virginia to Utah are in open rebellion, declaring they will no longer comply with the NCLB law, since it amounts to a cumbersome, questionable, and unfunded federal mandate.

Meanwhile, the education president's 2005 budget provides just enough money to allow Head Start (which is only one of the most successful education programs in history) to reach half of the eligible children. Also, the Early Head Start program is budgeted so low that it can serve only 5 percent of those eligible. That's a lot of children left behind.

Here's a cute one for you: Shouldn't schoolchildren be in good classrooms and safe buildings? *Well, of course,* you shout! But they're not. Our nation's school buildings are, on average, forty-two years old; leaking roofs and falling plaster are common, and a third of America's schools now use trailers as classrooms. The backlogged cost of bringing dilapidated school buildings up to par and providing adequate classrooms for every schoolchild is now calculated by the American Society of Engineers to be $127 billion.

❝ Where did this idea come from that everybody deserves free education? It comes from Moscow, from Russia. It comes straight out of the pit of hell. ❞

—*Texas State Representative* **Debbie Riddle**, *expressing the far-right-wing's understanding of history in the 2003 legislative session*

(Actually, the idea of free public education was spawned in America by such moderate to conservative thinkers as Horace Mann and John Dewey.)

Bush's latest budget freezes funding for school maintenance and new construction. He provides only $54 million—enough to build only six medium-size schools in a nation of need.

You say America can't afford $127 billion, Limbaugh breath? That's a mere *one tenth* of the $1.2 TRILLION that Bush intends to give to the richest Americans in tax cuts over the next ten years. Take back only one of those years, and every American kid could learn in a clean, well-lighted, safe classroom.

It's a fundamental question of whether we're going to base our nation's future on the wealthy few or the common good.

Forget Health Care, We're Going to Mars

Why is it that our national policy makers are so robustly optimistic and filled with such can-do enthusiasm when it comes to shoveling billions of our tax dollars into big federal projects favored by wealthy campaign donors, but fall into dismal depths of negativity and dispirited cries of no-can-do pessimism when it comes to paying for the things the majority of us Americans want and desperately need?

Take health care, a glaring national need not only for the 43 million people without any coverage, but also for the many millions more who have insurance policies that are so inadequate, expensive, and riddled with insurance company loopholes that their "coverage" is next to useless. The prestigious Institute of Medicine has just issued a report saying that our country has a swelling health-care crisis and that policy makers should respond with a universal program to provide affordable, high-quality health care to all.

How did policy makers respond? With a big "No way!" Tommy Thompson, secretary of health and human services, led the naysaying: "I just don't think it's in the cards," he maintains. "I don't think that, administratively or legislatively, it's feasible." This guy is America's top health-care official faced with a crucial issue that per-

❝We're going to lose a lot of kids from CHIP, but perhaps now their parents will go back to many of their private health-care plans.❞

[What about those who can't afford or are unable to get private insurance?]

❝There's always churches and clinics to help those who fall between the cracks.❞

—*Texas State Representative* **Leo Berman**, *explaining what will happen to the 200,000 poor children who will be kicked out of the Children's Health Insurance Program due to Republican budget cuts in 2003*

sonally affects the majority of Americans, yet he whimpers that good health care for everyone is simply beyond America's ability, so he won't even try for it.

Ironically, the institute's report and plea for action came the same day Bush announced that he wanted to spend unlimited billions of our tax dollars to build a space station on the moon and send astronauts to Mars. His political aides said the futuristic Mars shot was a reflection of Bush's optimistic nature.

How about we bring some of that optimism down to earth where we all live.

Reforming Nursing Home Rules

Here comes another sweet dollop of compassion from George W, this time directed at ill, vulnerable, and often-abused senior citizens who reside in nursing homes across the country.

The federal government regulates seventeen thousand of these nursing home operations, which get $39 billion a year in our tax money to care for 1.6 million elderly or disabled patients. Few industries as a whole have had such a sorry record of performance as this one. Hardly a month goes by without another scandal that reveals shocking levels of mistreatment by nursing home firms that squeeze unconscionable profits from sick old people by understaffing and undercaring. In 2000, the U.S. Department of Health and Human Services found that *most* nursing homes do not have enough employees to provide proper care.

The good news is that Mr. Compassionate Conservative came into office with a plan. It's called the "nursing home quality initiative." The bad news is that instead of relieving the pain of suffering patients, Bush's plan provided relief for the nursing home industry itself! Its lobbyists have long been crying that operators of these places are overregulated. This industry was an early and generous Bush financial backer, so he scratched their backs. He changed the rules to ease the standards for patient protection, eliminate a host of penalties for mistreating patients, and—one of George's favorite tricks—allow the companies to inspect themselves.

The Bushites, always compassionate toward corporate campaign contributors, say they want government to move away from an adversarial approach to a "collaborative" relationship with the industry. One part of their proposed sweetheart collaboration is to eliminate the policy of automatically punishing nursing homes that, on two consecutive biannual inspections, have been caught causing harm or immediate jeopardy to the patients.

Defending America from Canada

Dick Cheney, Rummy Rumsfeld, Colin Powell, and Condi Rice aren't the only fierce hawks in George W's warmongering government, and the Pentagon is not the only federal force that Bush has unleashed to attack a foreign foe in the name of defending "The Homeland." Here's the name of another hawkish generalissimo: Mark B. McClellan.

Who? OK, Mark's a dimmer light in George's galaxy of self-styled "tough guys and gals," but he's no less committed to BushCo's agenda of global empire, in which all other countries are expected to do our bidding . . . or else. Until recently, McClellan was Bush's commissioner of the Food and Drug Administration, whence he launched his own war against a rogue nation that, he claims, threatens the very safety of the American people. The name of this heinous assaulter? Canada.

Canada? A people so gentle that their national flag features a maple leaf? What threat are they?

Well, huffed Generalissimo McClellan, Canadian pharmacies sell prescription drugs at prices 30 to 50 percent cheaper than what the drug makers charge in America. So? Well, he said, on-line businesses in our country are allowing America's consumers to buy their medicines through Canada rather than paying the rip-off prices here in the homeland. So? Well, he sputters, the drug industry *DoesNotLikeThis,* so it must be stopped!

THANK YOU, JOHN

I'm sure you're wondering: In this matter of governmental loopiness over importing cheaper drugs from Canada, where's the Bushites' Caped Crusader of Loopiness, *John Ashcroft?* I'm pleased to report that he's been Johnny-on-the-spot.

Last year, he took time away from his assault on antiwar protestors to issue a Code Red Alert against a company called RxDepot. He brought the full legal forces of the federal government down on this small firm to try to quash its enterprising efforts to help Americans import medicines from Canada. It's good to know that our public servants are so vigilant in their determination to prevent us from paying less for prescription drugs.

Thus we have witnessed the remarkable sight of our FDA commissioner attacking our good neighbor to the north so the drug giants can keep overcharging Americans. Of course, McClellan claimed that it's for our own good, because those dastardly Canadians might be shipping unsafe drugs to us.

In response, the Canadians note that practically all of the medicines they ship are made by American companies under the FDA's own supervision, and that Canada has excellent drug safety laws, at least as good as those in the USA.

You've got to love these laissez-faire ideologues who keep insisting against overwhelming evidence to the contrary that the magic potion for all of our economic ills is globalization. Yet in the case of prescription drugs, these very same zealots have flip-flopped, vehemently arguing *against* globalization. The reason for their abandonment of ideology is that this particular piece of globalization would benefit not corporations, but patients.

The drug giants have gone bananas on this issue, enlisting the White House, the Republican leadership in Congress, and some Democrats—people who are usually die-hard globalizers—to try to keep our borders closed to cheaper medicines.

Last year they mounted an all-out lobbying offensive to bottle up the Market Access Act, which would have empowered American consumers to import approved prescription medicines at the best price globally, even though a majority of Congress favored it.

Later in the year, proponents of cheaper drug prices attached a consumer importation provision to Bush's bill to provide some drug benefits for Medicare patients. Oh, the uproar! Industry lobbyists shrieked louder than Little Richard and, PDQ, that little provision was taken into the back rooms of Congress and stomped to death, leaving us Americans captive to drug company gouging. For his loyalty to the gougers, Mark McClellan got promoted by Bush from the FDA to the post of running America's Medicare program.

CONGRESS'S PRESCRIPTION

Gosh, words fail me. I can't begin to describe the level of pride I feel for Congress, which has recently stepped forth boldly to meet the crying health needs of a group of America's senior citizens: themselves.

Thanks to sparse media coverage you probably don't know that our congressional leaders quietly passed a special drug benefit bill for a select group of retirees that—lo and behold— happens to include them. Their benefits package is also far more generous than what they had doled out so stingily for ordinary, everyday, run-of-the-mill seniors in the much-ballyhooed Medicare "reform" they passed last year.

For example, retired members of Congress will pay no additional premium or deductible for their drug coverage, while other retirees are assessed an extra $420 out-of-pocket annual premium and a $250 deductible. Representative Pete Stark (D-Calif.), disgusted with this privileged treatment, said: "This bill says, 'We take care of our own, and to hell with the average American.'"

I've got a simple prescription for reforming America's health-care system: We'll take the same thing Congress gets.

Yet this fight for fairness is a long way from over. Several governors are openly defying the Bush administration's flagrant whoring for the drug giants, a majority in Congress (including many Republicans) continue to oppose the industry and the White House, and consumers themselves have taken matters into their own hands, finding ways to import an estimated billion dollars' worth of cheaper drugs from Canada this year.

Why Drugs Cost So Much

As anyone who does much fishing can tell you, sometimes you can get snagged on your own hook.

This has recently happened to America's big drug makers, who have long tried to justify the outrageous prices they charge by hooking those prices to their need to do a lot of research and development work. Oh, wail the pharmaceutical executives to those of us who want to curb these soaring prices, if you do that we'll have to slash our research budgets and then there'll be epidemics and people will die and you'll be to blame.

The consumer watchdog group Families USA, however, decided to examine the industry's hook up close, checking to see if the high prices really are attached to R&D. In a word, "uh-uh." Based on the drug corporations' own annual reports, the group found that the firms that market the fifty most-prescribed drugs to seniors actually spend *twice as much* on advertising, marketing, and corporate bureaucracy than they do on research and development. Moreover, the net profits of such giants as Merck, Bristol-Myers Squibb, Abbott Labs, and Eli Lilly dwarf their expenditures for R&D. Indeed, the drug industry by far reaps the highest rate of profit of any U.S. industry, with margins that are four times greater than the average Fortune 500 company.

And while the CEOs of these outfits pretend to worry about

THE PHARMACEUTICAL CORPORATIONS . . .

- Spend $200 million a year on Washington lobbying
- Have 134 lobbying firms on their payroll
- Employ a total of 625 registered lobbyists
  (*this is 90 more lobbyists than there are members of Congress!*)

their research budgets, they are personally hauling millions of dollars out of their companies. In 2001, just in stock payments—not counting their multimillion-dollar salaries and bonuses—these guys made a killing, including $130 million worth of stock compensation to Pfizer's chief, $181 million to the honcho of Merck, and $227 million to the head of Bristol-Myers. They rake in these paychecks while their rip-off pricing policies force seniors across the country to have to choose between medicine and food.

Social Security Works

Gather 'round me, children, and I'll tell you a story of progressive progress.

In 1939, *two thirds* of America's senior citizens lived their "golden years" in cold, hard poverty. Just a decade later, that percentage was down to half. By 1959, it was only one third. Today, the number is less than 10 percent.

That's progress. What's progressive about it is that this decline in poverty is the result of the New Deal's passage of our nation's landmark social security program.

Yes, the very same program now under attack by Wall Street wolves, George W, Alan Greenspan, and congressional opportunists of both parties—all insisting that social security is doomed to failure and facing an imminent financial crisis.

Horsedooties. First, this is a program that actually works, providing a modicum of income so our gray-haired citizens have a basic level of decent living when their earning years are over. Second, social security is a model of efficiency, taking only one single percent in administrative costs. Compare that to the insurance corporations that suck out one third of our health-care dollars to pay for their corporate bureaucracies, executive salaries, marble palaces, and advertising.

But, no, cry the Chicken Littlers, social security is going broke!

Broke, I say, broke! Chill, C.L. In the first place, the system is now taking in way more money than it spends. The trust fund is running a multibillion-dollar surplus that Bush (like every president since LBJ) joyously raids to pay for his current profligate spending spree and tax cuts, even as he cries crocodile tears for the fund. He takes cash from social security and leaves IOUs for future generations of taxpayers to make good.

Yet even with the raids, the system is fully financed and absolutely sound through at least 2042. Name me a corporation that can claim that! And with only some tweaks and a modest infusion of money (which could easily be covered by canceling some of George's impetuous tax giveaways to the millionaire class), the system could maintain its current level of benefits to retirees for *the next seventy-five years.*

Yet the Bushites, on behalf of Wall Street finaglers, seek to privatize this public treasure, pushing people to put their social security nest egg into the stock market. Hello! These are the same investment geniuses who only four years ago would have advised you to invest in Enron—a stock that fell from $97 a share to 57 cents in only one year!

Aside from that, there's another little catch that Bush & Company does not advertise: fees. The big Wall Street investment firms

---

THIS BUD'S FOR YOU

In 2002, an investment advisory on the Internet noted that if you had bought $1,000 worth of Enron stock the year before, your investment would've shrunk to $16.50. If you'd bought $1,000 worth of WorldCom stock, you'd have had only $5 left from your investment. But . . . if you'd bought $1,000 worth of Budweiser (the beer, not the stock), quaffed all the beer, and cashed in the cans for the ten-cent deposit, you would have $214. So, the prudent investment strategy is clear: Drink heavily and recycle. And don't let anyone put your social security money in Wall Street's hands.

are drooling over the possibility of getting their fat hands on social security because they'll pocket billions of dollars a year from the fees they would charge every time they buy or sell a stock with your money. These fees would come straight off the top of your social security account, drastically cutting the returns that you'd get.

To try to give blue-ribbon cover to this grab for our public retirement fund, George appointed a Social Security Reform Commission shortly after he took office. Forget any impartial report coming from this stacked deck of a commission—all members had to agree in advance to back Bush's pet proviso of privatization. Who are these people?

- Co-chairing the commission was Richard Parsons, top exec for media giant AOL Time Warner, where Parsons ran a job scam that tried to deny pension benefits to employees there. He got caught, was sued, and Time Warner had to pay $5.5 million to compensate the workers he tried to short.

- There were also three former Congress critters on board, each of whom favors privatizing social security, raising our retirement age to as high as seventy, and cutting our monthly benefits. Hey, it's no hair off their butts, since all three have the Cadillac congressional pensions that'll pay them millions in retirement, so they won't even need social security.

- Four other commissioners came straight from the Wall Street world that will pocket the social security cash that would flow from privatization, while another four hail from right-wing think tanks that have long proselytized for privatization—and are financed by corporations that would profit from it.

Notice who's missing. You! The two thirds of Americans who count on social security for retirement income were not represented. Unsurprisingly, Bush's rigged commission issued a report in 2002 calling for various versions of privatization. It's still laying there on George's shelf, ready to be dusted off if he wins in November.

Here's my suggestion: Don't accept the "reforms" of any commission unless it's made up of people who will actually need social security when they retire.

Edison Comes A-Cropper

> **"** *Public education is the balance wheel of society.* **"**
>
> *—Horace Mann, 1848*

Edison Schools, Inc., has become the Blanche Dubois of the movement to corporatize America's public schools. Blanche was the fragile character in *A Streetcar Named Desire* who said, "I've always depended on the kindness of strangers."

In the mid-nineties, Edison was a cocky company. Its executives were blustering that America's public schools needed less "public" and more "corporate"—more of the managerial know-how and bottom-line business efficiency that an outfit like theirs could deliver. Give us your educational money, they told school districts, and we'll by God give you back academic excellence, plus we'll pay a sweet profit to our investors. Wall Street was dazzled, throwing money at Edison, while equally dazzled school officials threw their kids at the company, which quickly became the largest commercial operator of public schools.

But running schools turns out to be a bit harder than the corporatizers figured. Edison has not outperformed publicly managed schools, even though it has gotten more money per student for its schools, and it has never made an annual profit, losing another $25 million last year. Indeed, like Blanche, Edison has always relied on the kindness of strangers—or, in its case, relied on bedazzled investors who've been kind enough to overlook hundreds of millions of dollars in losses, skyrocketing overhead, and shady insider dealings.

By 2002, however, the glitter was gone. The corporation was drawing more critics than cheerleaders for its educational performance, it was losing contracts in several states, it was mired in heavy debt, administrative costs were soaring at its posh Manhattan headquarters on Fifth Avenue, and its stock price had plummeted from $35 a share in early 2001 to about $1.25. Wall Street analysts quit recommending the stock to investors, and Edison faced the ignominy of being tossed off the NASDAQ listing of stocks.

Last fall, Edison's once-flamboyant founder, Chris Whittle, tucked his tail between his legs, merged the battered company with an investment outfit, and converted Edison from a high-flying, publicly traded corporation to a privately held firm.

So much for corporate efficiency and know-how. If you can't run a company, how're you going to run something as infinitely more complex as a public school?

Teaching Commercialism

Remember the field trips you took in elementary school—maybe to the fire department, a farm, a radio station, or other places where you learned a bit about how things work?

Well, now those old-fashioned field trips are being updated . . . and *commercialized*. Why send kids to the farm when we can send them to Petco, the national chain that sells animals to kids? Teachers bring classes into the local Petco outlet, where the kids hear a talking parrot, see an exotic lizard, pet a puppy . . . and get coupons for free goldfish. "By the weekend," says a Petco official, "at least ten [of the kids] will be here with their families to show them what they got to see—and to redeem the coupon."

Good grief, they're turning field trips into come-ons for tiny shoppers, teaching the crass art of consumerism. If we let this go on, they'll be taking the tykes into toy stores next. Too late. Toys 'R' Us is already hosting school field trips, offering a "mighty minds" tour of the store that lets students use the toys, puzzles, art supplies, and other goodies for sale there.

THE SHAME OF RE-SEGREGATION

"Let us be dissatisfied," said Dr. Martin Luther King Jr., "until the dark yesterdays of segregated schools will be transformed into bright tomorrows of quality integrated education."

Thanks to the broad civil rights movement and the prevailing goodwill of the American people, our country strived for years to reach that bright tomorrow. And while we never quite got there, we made great strides—and at least we were trying as a nation. But then stuff happened.

In the late 1980s, legislatures and courts cynically abandoned King's vision, halting our decades-long commitment to integration. As a result, according to a study released this year by Harvard University researchers, the trend rapidly reversed, and most white students today have little contact with black and Latino students. In southern states, 70 percent of black students are now in predominantly black schools. In western states, some 80 percent of Latino students are in predominantly Latino schools—twice as many as in 1968, when Dr. King was assassinated.

It's time for all of us to be dissatisfied again.

This branding of young minds has become its own industry, with companies like the Field Trip Factory operating as go-betweens to link local schools with corporate chains. This one company set up 3,300 of these student tours at Petco stores last school year.

Obviously, the chains get access to impressionable little buyers who're conveniently delivered to them by their teachers—no advertising campaign could match that. But what do the schools get? In these times of cutbacks in school budgets, they get a prepackaged cheap outing for their classes. As one school official happily exclaimed about the corporate jaunts: "We can provide kids with experiences at no cost."

No cost? The cost is in the integrity of the educational experience and in the commercialization of our children.

Higher Education for All

Given what you've seen in recent times, I know you're not going to believe this, but here it is: Once upon a time, Congress occasionally did the right thing, in the right way.

Ludicrous! you shout. *Tell me that pigs fly, that the sun will rise in the west tomorrow, that Britney Spears is a serious musical talent, but tell me no fables about that gang of thieves under the Capitol dome.*

It's true. As evidence, I point you to the Congress of 1944, which passed what became known as the GI Bill. It opened up higher education, previously the exclusive enclave of elites, to masses of Americans. Admittedly, Congress's motive was not altruism, but panic. Some 14 million soldiers were about to return from World War II and there were simply no jobs for them. It could be quite explosive to have millions of mostly young and largely unskilled men milling around, most of whom had ambition, many of whom were coming home with lots of experience in how to use guns.

Better to channel this mass of energy, aspiration, and testosterone into . . . what? The answer was college, trade schools, and training programs. The GI Bill allowed veterans who could meet the academic qualifications to go to the school of their choice for up to four years—*free!* They received grants of up to $500, which in that day would cover all tuition, books, fees, etc. Plus, they got living stipends of up to $50 a month.

It was a major public investment in ordinary people—not a trickle-down approach but a percolate-up—*and it worked.*

The total cost was $14.5 billion—$1,860 per vet. There was a huge payoff for our nation from this investment—a 1988 congressional study of one group educated under the GI Bill found that every dollar invested produced a $7 increase in our nation's output. Also, as happens after a good, soaking two-inch spring rain, many flowers bloomed across our country as a result of this showering of public funds on America's grassroots:

- The growth that the GI Bill stimulated in higher-educational enrollment fueled a broad expansion of colleges, trade schools, and other institutions, with many new institutions and campuses reaching for the first time into inner-city and rural communities, putting advanced education within physical and economic reach of people who otherwise might not have had the opportunity or even considered the possibility of more schooling.

- The boom in enrollment also meant a boom in construction jobs, and new educational facilities created other jobs—from teachers to janitors, administrators to cafeteria workers.

- The college and university experience was dramatically democratized, broadened, and deepened as students from working-class and farm backgrounds were afforded the chance to go in large numbers to what had been havens for the elite.

Here's a big idea for today's political consideration: Let's do that again. Let's revisit the concept of the GI Bill, but expand it to every American. Anyone who can meet the academic qualifications should have their tuition, fees, and other educational expenses covered, plus a reasonable living stipend, for education and training beyond high school. Yes, free education for all.

The Powers That Be constantly scold us about the importance of education, repeatedly pointing out that the key to personal advance-

> More than 7 million vets were trained during the twelve-year life of the GI Bill:
> —2.2 million went to college
> —3.5 million went to trade and technical schools
> —1.4 million got on-the-job training
> —700,000 got farm training

A PUBLIC UNIVERSITY ACTS LIKE ONE

At a time when the very concept of the "public good" is being bashed and dashed, what a joy it is to get a bit of good news from Chapel Hill, North Carolina.

Officials at at the University of North Carolina have taken a stand to make a university education more universal for the people of the state—particularly for students from families of the working poor. In a first for public universities, UNC announced last year that it will cover these students' full cost, including room and board, of attending the university—a total of about $13,000 a year for each student. In turn, the students will work on campus ten to twelve hours a week.

"College should be possible for everyone who can make the grade, regardless of family income," says the UNC chancellor. Yet surveys show that the rapidly rising cost of attending college (up 200 percent in the past twenty years) and the fear of having to amass too much of a debt load on them and their families are now preventing about half of our country's academically qualified low-income students from attending.

So UNC has made an important and bold decision not to abandon those who are being priced out. The chancellor says simply that this policy is "an expression of our values at this university."

ment and to the advancement of our country in today's global "knowledge economy" is advanced education. High school no longer cuts it, we're told; you must get higher skills and knowledge for the twenty-first century.

Yet increasingly, not only are poor folks priced out of this opportunity, but so is the middle class. College has become a sinkhole of debt for those who can borrow to go (U.S. Public Interest Research Group finds that two thirds of college students now graduate with loan debts averaging $17,000), and those with no capacity to borrow are simply locked out.

As with the GI Bill, our modern-day initiative should not be limited to the pursuit of university degrees. "Higher" education means just that—higher than high school. Advanced educational opportunities ought to be as populist as possible, letting people choose for themselves what works for them. Whether the end result is a lab coat or a chef's toque, whether you learn Web site design in a community college or auto design in a technical institute, whether you study nursing or woodworking, whether you're granted a B.A. in accounting or earn certification as a master organic farmer—our society benefits, for you have more knowledge than before and more potential to contribute to the common good.

Free higher education is also a natural fit for our new global order, a fast-spinning world in which employees can forget about such old-fashioned niceties as corporate loyalty and job security, no matter how much of yourself you've dedicated to the company. Washington and Wall Street tell us that we must expect to get dumped frequently and scramble for new work, usually requiring higher skills.

OK, so in a wealthy nation like ours, which has become the world model for this new chaotic economy, let's lead the way in providing secure footing for our people by making sure that an infrastructure of free education and training is always in place. If this is the way the new world is going to be, let's adjust for that world. To do less would be a damnable failure of leadership.

The naysayers will shriek: *"Where are you going to get the money for such a massive public investment?"* Get it from where it went. The total cost of the GI Bill was about $80 billion in today's money. Washington has already frittered away $95 billion on the

Star Wars boondoggle and plans to spend hundreds of billions more. On national security grounds alone, education for all beats the bejeezus out of this silly system.

If we're going to be stingy, let's get downright miserly about doling out more multibillion-dollar military contracts to Halliburton, giving a $257 million tax rebate to Enron, and generally shoveling our hard-earned dollars into corporate coffers.

It's a matter of what We the People want to do. As we learned after September 11, the money can be found to do whatever needs to be done—and even for what doesn't need to be done.

But the bottom line on higher education for all is more than economic, for it represents a truly populist vision that embraces the democratic aspirations of America's workaday majority. It empowers people directly, letting them decide when, where, and what advanced education they'll get. It abandons the elitist notion that higher education is reserved for the top tier and respects the dignity of all kinds of educational pursuits.

Why Libraries Matter

For me, the truest symbol of America's great democratic spirit is not to be found in the formal and imposing edifices of our republic—the White House, the Capitol, or the monuments to Washington, Jefferson, Lincoln, and others. Rather, I look to the much more modest, diverse, dispersed, and welcoming expressions of our nation's egalitarian ideals: our public libraries.

Libraries in particular embody the collective story of a place, which makes each library richly unique. Yet the wonderful uniqueness of each is made more wonderful by a crucial underlying sameness, which is that they all exist to serve *the common good* of the community.

This is why libraries matter in a way that, say, a Barnes & Noble cannot. These public institutions are democratic by nature, making their resources open to all, thus giving legs to America's historic pursuit of egalitarianism. As James Madison put it:

A popular government, without popular information, or the means of acquiring it, is but a prologue to a farce or a tragedy; or perhaps both. Knowledge will forever govern ignorance; and a people who mean to be their own governors must arm themselves with the power which knowledge gives.

I'm a beneficiary of the public purpose and the community goodwill that libraries represent. I was born and raised in Denison, Texas, seventy-five miles due north of Dallas, right on the Oklahoma border. Aside from being the birthplace of Dwight Eisenhower, our town of railroad workers, Main Street merchants, truck drivers, farmers, and other regular folk once had the dubious distinction of being the largest community in Texas without a public library.

Luckily, however, before I was born, the citizenry decided that if Denison was to be any kind of proper town, it needed the anchor of a library. It's said that a local businessman, Clarence Johnson, sparked the movement in 1935 after he grew tired of having to drive ten miles to our rival city of Sherman to get access to its library's reference books.

In the old barn-raising spirit, all sorts of people joined the effort, though they didn't have to build a barn, since Denison's wealthiest family, the Munsons, offered one of their old homes rent-free for two years. This fine building had been the first brick house built in our town, so housing the library there added both cachet and seriousness to the cause.

The town held a fund-raising carnival at the high school. Boy Scouts assisted in collecting books and magazines. The high school librarian, Ms. Pauline Jordan, directed the cataloging, and, on November 22, 1935, the library formally opened with a "book and silver tea" attended by 250 proud Denisonians. The book collection totaled 1,200 volumes.

The public response was so strong that the voluntary library did not have the operating funds and books to meet the need. So an election was called and the good citizens of our town voted to raises their property taxes and adequately fund a full-time public library. Bear in mind, this was in the midst of the Depression!

By the time I was old enough to get my own check-out card, Denison's library had moved into a first-rate modern building with air-conditioning and thousands of books that brought the entire world to my fingertips. All of this was available to me because others thought that it was a matter of providing for the common good. My parents, Lillie and "High" Hightower, had been part of this community development, voting all along the way to tax themselves in order to make such a possibility available to the people, especially including those who couldn't afford to buy books.

Actually, my folks might have been considered likely to oppose the availability of free books and magazines, since they ran a newsstand and a wholesale business selling books and magazines. But they believed that a library was good for all, and that what was good for all would be good for them . . . and their three boys.

This is the true spirit of America, the public spirit that the rest of the world rarely glimpses, and that we're rarely shown by our own media and political powers. This is the spirit we must highlight, tap into . . . and build our democratic future on.

The Book Thing

In a culture that refers to sport's figures as "heroes" and treats movie stars as "role models," I relish people like Russell Wattenberg, founder and chief scrounger of a Baltimore store called the Book Thing. What is unique about the Book Thing is that its books are absolutely free—indeed, adamantly free. "THIS IS A FREE

BOOK," Wattenberg gleefully rubber-stamps into each volume, adding emphatically: "Not for Resale."

His determinedly anticommercial approach to book dealing started some six years ago when he was tending bar at Dougherty's Pub. Some schoolteachers who frequented Dougherty's told him about students too poor to afford books, which led Wattenberg on his first foray to find freebies. He was surprised at how easy it was to get a batch of books for the students . . . and thus was born the Book Thing.

Now he's a full-time scrounger, operating out of a basement store down the street from Dougherty's. The Book Thing is open only on weekends, with Wattenberg spending the rest of his week either gathering books or driving his book van to schools, homeless shelters, and any other place where people might welcome free reading material. He gives away hundreds of thousands of discarded books each year, ranging from mint-condition coffee-table volumes to tattered classics. The enterprise is guided by a neighborhood board of directors who are regulars at the pub, and some thirty volunteers help him run it.

He says people are not only eager readers but eager donors as well. He particularly loves the subversiveness of Baltimore's librarians: While city regulators officially prohibit them from donating their used books, he says he gets "anonymous calls telling me fifty boxes will be in an alleyway at five o'clock."

Where Did Ranger George Go?

When you go into America's national parks, your eyes and soul soak up the experience—majestic mountains, timeless forests, breathtaking canyons, expansive seashores.

But if you look around, you'll also notice something not so spectacular: rotting facilities, fewer visitor hours, closed-off areas, fewer rangers—all signs of a phenomenal national asset being allowed to deteriorate. Why is this happening? Where is our national leadership?

As a presidential candidate, George W expressed indignation at the failure to maintain such a priceless system. In 2000, he staged a campaign media event with the soaring Cascade Mountains as his backdrop, warning in outrage that our national parks are "at the breaking point," and he vowed to voters that he'd eliminate the $5 billion backlog in needed maintenance within five years, restoring the system to its proper grandeur.

Four years later, Ranger George is nowhere to be seen. The national maintenance need is now $6 billion, and in his entire tenure, Bush has allocated less than $300 million to address the still-growing backlog—a mere 5 percent of what's needed.

Our Ellis Island Park, for example, a shrine to America's historic ethnic diversity, now has some twenty deteriorating structures in serious need of repair, and caretakers have to scramble to maintain irreplaceable artifacts in rooms with leaking roofs and peeling plaster. Park employees elsewhere are frustrated by such ever-worsening conditions as the broken pipes in Yellowstone National Park that caused a spill of ten thousand gallons of raw sewage—the kind of thing that could sour the experience of watching Old Faithful spew into the sky.

Bush even slashed 40 percent of the repair budget for the very same mountain park that he had used as a political backdrop four years ago. And instead of expanding our public parks, as every president for the last century has done, George allowed national park space to shrink by 187,000 acres in 2002 alone.

He also cut the overall repair budget for western parks by 28 percent, diverting much of this money to his right-wing, antigovernment goal of privatizing our public system. His Competitive Sourcing Initiative forces the park service to review all staff positions and consider allowing corporate profiteers to replace

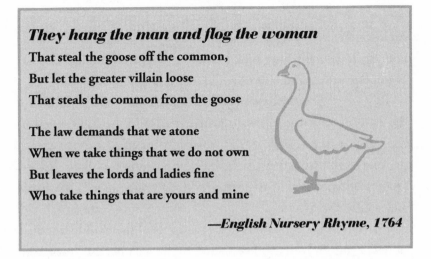

They hang the man and flog the woman

That steal the goose off the common,

But let the greater villain loose

That steals the common from the goose

The law demands that we atone

When we take things that we do not own

But leaves the lords and ladies fine

Who take things that are yours and mine

—English Nursery Rhyme, 1764

about seventeen hundred experienced workers with poorly trained low-wage workers.

Teddy Roosevelt would be ashamed . . . but then George is no Teddy, despite trying to pose as one during election years.

The Corporate Takeover of Our Water

The ideologues and greedheads who brought us the fairy tale of energy deregulation and the Ponzi scheme of Enron are aggressively pushing for deregulation and privatization of one of life's essentials: water. They are determined to turn our water supplies and systems—a vital public resource—into just another commodity for traders and speculators, a private plaything for personal profiteering.

In just the past few years, transnational conglomerates have already privatized all or parts of the water systems of Atlanta, Berlin, Buenos Aires, Bolivia, Casablanca, Charleston, Chattanooga, Ghana, Houston, Jacksonville, Jersey City, Lexington, New Orleans, Peoria, Ontario, San Francisco, and many other places.

It amounts to a corporate "water rush." In our country, private control has rapidly become global control: The largest U.S. firm, American Water Works, was swallowed up by RWE of Germany; Suez Lyonnaise of France took our second biggest company, United Water Resources; and Vivendi of France grabbed U.S. Filter.

Two years ago, *Fortune* magazine exulted that water "will be to the 21st century what oil was to the 20th." And the magazine was thrilled that "the liquid everybody needs . . . is going private, creating one of the world's great business opportunities." Four factors are powering this rush to privatization: scarcity, greed, ideology, and political weaseliness.

The World Bank predicts that two thirds of the world's population will run short of adequate water in the next twenty years. You might think that the sheer scariness of this scarcity would prompt policy makers to focus on such goals as protecting the purity of the aqua we have, pushing rational conservation, and promoting the long-term public interest in this irreplaceable resource.

Whoa there, Pollyanna! You forget greed. Speculators look at the looming scarcity of a substance that no one can do without and think, "Wow, if I could control that, I could make a killing." Suddenly, the unsexy task of piping in water and piping out sewage became a hot prospect.

This coincided nicely with the corporate right wing's ideological zealotry for the mumbo jumbo of deregulation and privatization. Not only can conglomerates do everything better than a democratic government can, goes their religious mantra, but they firmly believe that today's global corporations are magical kingdoms run by new-economy wunderkinds.

This is where the political weasels come in. From the mid-seventies to the present, just about every politician from mayoral to presidential candidates of both major parties have caved in to the privatization ideologues, campaigning and governing as tight-fisted, no-more-taxes, business-minded conservatives.

So local pols have frittered away public funds on building flashy sports palaces for privately owned teams, and national pols have cooked up trillion-dollar tax giveaways to the richest people in the country—and all of the pols have let America's crucial water systems fall apart. To fix decades-old leaking pipes, sputtering pumps, and the other faltering parts of the water infrastructure will require an estimated $11 billion a year more than governments are now spending.

Faced with this unpleasantness, weaseling politicians have simply escalated their weaseling. Rather than being straight with people by saying, "Look, we've got to get our public house in order," the pols at all levels have thrown open the doors of our house to any corporate flimflammer with a medicine wagon, a talking pony, and a bottle of that old magic elixir: privatization!

In case after case where corporate water vandals have taken the handle to the public pump, folks have found themselves left with skyrocketing bills, foul water, lousy service, nonfunctioning fire hydrants—and no control over the culprits.

Consider United Water Resources, which had humble origins as the Hackensack Water Company. In the mid-nineties, however, the company got ambitious, dressing up in the sleeker corporate name of UWR Inc. and going on an expansionist binge that quickly made it the second-largest corporate water fiefdom in the United States, before UWR itself was swallowed by Suez Lyonnaise. The company and its executives have hauled in millions in profits and personal gains from its privatization adventures, but its customers have been soaked.

In Atlanta, UWR promised dramatic cost savings, which it proceeded to get by whacking the city's water staff from 731 employees to only 327. Among the "savings" this produced:

- Debris and rust started turning up in residents' water. At first, UWR honchos denied there was a problem. But, hey, the tap water was brown! Even then, it was four months before the company did anything.

- Fire hydrants started coming up dry or inoperative. Again, executives tried to deny that there was a problem. Then, when it was pointed out that this was life-and-death stuff, UWR tried to shift the blame (and the cost), saying that after the company repaired or replaced a hydrant, it was the city's responsibility to test it to see if it actually worked.
- Complaints piled up about impossibly slow service on everything from repairing leaks to installing water meters.

In the 2002 mayoral election, Shirley Franklin made UWR the central issue in her campaign, pledging to give the company the boot and restore public control if she was elected. She was . . . and she did.

Water privatization doesn't work because its fundamental promises are lies. Far from bringing "market forces" to bear, these corporations are handed a monopoly and face no competition. Wielding monopoly power, they slash staff, lower wages, compromise service, cut corners on quality, skimp on long-term investment, raise rates—and call this "efficiency." Any savings derived from these tactics are routed into extravagant executive-pay packages, luxurious corporate headquarters, bureaucracy for the parent conglomerate, lavish advertising and lobbying budgets, and profits. All of this is done behind closed doors, for these private empires are not subject to the open-access and disclosure rules of public agencies. Then, when the peasants rebel, the faraway CEO dispatches an army of PR flacks and lawyers, overwhelming the financial resources available to local citizens and governments.

Now, the White House and Congress are ratcheting up their privatization push here at home with a sneak attack called the Water Investment Act of 2002. Despite its boring title, HR 1560 contains a stick of dynamite in it. Part of the bill says that a local

THE ENRON EXAMPLE

As Enron taught us, corporations are adept at hiding their financial shenanigans in a labyrinth of offshore accounts. Water corporations would be no different, totally befuddling local officials who are supposed to monitor them.

Take the case of Azurix, a high-flying water privatizer. It's not really a company but a convoluted consortium of more than fifty limited partnerships and interlocking subsidiaries created in the secretive tax haven of the Cayman Islands. Its creator was none other than Enron. Now it's owned by RWE.

water project in your city cannot get federal financing unless the local government "has considered" privatizing your water system. Upgrading and expanding water systems is hugely expensive, and cities must have federal support to do the job, but HR 1560 would make this funding conditional on whether cities consider turning over their water to private corporations.

Substituting private interest for public interest has not exactly been serendipitous in the energy sector, so why in hell should we give corporations (foreign-based ones, at that) our water? At least government entities are supposed to be legally and politically responsible to We the People. But corporations maintain (and the law agrees) that they are responsible solely to their big stockholders—an elite group that invariably includes the CEO. In water, the stockholders' interests will inevitably conflict with the public's.

Water is one of life's necessities, which is why we must treat it as part of our commons—the wealth that we hold in trust so it will be there for all of us, not only for today but for all of our tomorrows as well.

The Big Muddy of Corporatization

It wasn't long ago that we first put a toe into the Big Muddy of corporatization, letting brand-name corporations plaster their commercial logos on our tax-paid public facilities. Then we were quickly ankle-deep in these murky waters, then knee-deep, and now we're at least butt-deep, with the Big Muddy still rising.

For example, hardly a sports stadium exists in America today without the blare and glare of some corporate brand, as though the private huckster owns the place. For a fee (which itself is tax deductible), corporations like FedEx, MCI, BankOne, and even the executive sleazes of an outfit like Enron can grab the naming rights to buildings that the people built, using them as their private billboards. After branding our stadiums, the corporate name game moved to concert halls, museums . . . and we just keep getting deeper.

What is the price of a city's soul?

The top bid so far is $166 million. That's the sum that one company has paid to get corporate branding rights to New York City. In accepting the cold cash, Mayor Michael Bloomberg has callously changed this great city's slogan from the Big Apple . . . to the Big Snapple—having now made the British-owned beverage conglomerate the official drink of New York.

The Snapple deal is but step one of a sweeping and smarmy sell-off of the proud city's soul to assorted brand-name hucksters. To handle the devilish deals, Bloomberg has even hired a chief marketing officer, who blithely proclaims that "This is the start of a select number of really high-quality partnerships."

High quality? Check it out. For its cash, Snapple will get the exclusive right to place its vending machines in all city properties, starting with New York's twelve hundred public schools. The claim is that Snapple's fruit blends, YooHoo drinks, canned water, and iced tea are better for kids than, say, Coca-Cola, which has been banned from the city's schools for nutritional reasons.

But hold your empty-calorie, sugar-loaded concoctions right there, say nutritionists. It turns out that Snapple's fruit drinks have even more calories and sugar than Coca-Cola does! The Center for Science in the Public Interest reports that the Snapple drinks are "pretty much the same as a 12-ounce Coke." And as for Snapple's cans of water, one nutrition leader wonders why children are being charged to get a simple drink of H_2O: "Water is a right," she says, adding that "New York City is supposed to have the best [tap] water and we're asking children to pay $1 for [Snapple water]?"

Mayor Bloomberg, however, is a billionaire corporate creature who can't even begin to grasp the concept of free water. He says, "I don't think in this day and age we can take vending machines, or should, out of the schools."

Show a little spine, Mayor!

These days, commercial creativity is not defined as building a better mousetrap, but by hucksters finding yet another way to intrude into our quiet, to shove their way into our heads for no more noble purpose than to hawk, say, another pill for some problem we didn't know we had.

YACKETY-YAK TAXI

Save! *Free!*

Ever had overtalkative cabdrivers? You can forget about them, because they won't be able to get a word in edgewise thanks to such aptly named firms as Pointblank Medium and Captiveads. In Boston, Las Vegas, and elsewhere, they're installing video screens on the backs of drivers' seats so they can fire a nonstop loop of ads point-blank at you, literally holding you captive to corporate chatter.

AN ODE TO ALTIMA

Are you irritated by movie theaters that force you to watch several minutes of ads before getting to the film that you *paid* to see?

Well, beware: Nissan has upped the irritation level. At some movies, as the ad for Nissan's Altima rolls, several people hired by Nissan jump out of their seats and shout lines of poetry! It makes you wish you had a slingshot.

The latest contribution to the cacophony comes from Captivate Network, Inc., which has come up with a way to make a simple elevator ride annoying. Thanks to exciting advances in the science of wireless technology, it is now possible for outfits like Captivate to fill your thirty-second ride with: advertising videos. Yes, as you glide up to put in another day's work in your cubicle, you can be blessed by a yammering pitch for Right Guard, Starbucks, or Rolaids.

Captivate Inc.'s elevator ads are merely the tip of the commercialization iceberg for a Brave New World of Advertising that calls itself the "outernet industry." It sees all space outside the home as potential places for capturing consumer's ears and eyeballs for advertisers. This merciless industry is targeting doctors' offices, movie lobbies, commuter trains, convenience stores—even ski lifts! Already, Wal-Mart, Best Buy, and 7-Eleven are putting out-of-home advertising screens in their stores.

The *Los Angeles Times* reports that "The industry operates on a simple principle: Find out where consumers are gathering and put a screen in their faces." The possibilities are boundless—restrooms, bank drive-throughs, bus stops, golf tees, public parks, and along the boardwalks at the seashore. They can literally install this technology in tree trunks or on neighborhood fences, so we need never be more than a few seconds from the next product pitch.

The head of one of these outernet firms claims they're doing us a favor: "If you're standing in line waiting for a Big Mac and fries, you've got nothing else to do." Yes we do! We could think beautiful thoughts, hear some music, take tiny Yoga breaks . . . or plot revenge against the crass commercializers of our world.

The very idea of advertisers is to intrude into your head, doing whatever it takes to get there and plant a brand name like some alien pod of commercialization. Take Toyota. Last year it paid $100 million for branding rights to the pro-basketball stadium in Houston.

In announcing the plans for "branding" this public stadium, a Toyota honcho said, "It's not meant to be intrusive." Oh? This taxpayer-built facility will now be called the *Toyota Center,* it'll be covered inside and out with *Toyota*'s logo and ads, its lounge will be named *Lexus Lounge,* its parking garage will be named for *Toyota's Tundra* trucks, it will have *Toyota* vehicles positioned prominently throughout the arena, and there'll be a *Toyota* sales office at the games, staffed with sales reps hawking the cars.

Then there's the new public monorail system in Las Vegas. Its naming rights are being sold to corporations that'll plaster the place with their logos and ads—as though they own it.

First to buy into this monorail was Nextel, the phone huckster. For $50 million, it will have one of the system's trains covered with Nextel corporate colors, name, logo, and other promos. One of the monorail's train stops will be named the Nextel station, complete with a store, and a "Nexpert bar" staffed with employees promoting products. Yet Nextel's VP for marketing says, "I'm sensitive to the issue of overcommercialization."

Yeah, like a hog is sensitive to overeating. You want sensitive? The ad agency peddling the people's monorail to corporate hucksters says it doesn't see the function of the public system to be transportation but "transpertainment."

Take me now, Lord, I've lived too long.

Budgeting for Class Warfare

Am I the only one who thinks it's curious that people calling themselves "fiscal conservatives" are chugalugging federal money like frat boys bingeing on Ripple wine?

The Reaganauts did this to us twenty years ago, and now the Bushites (some of them the same people—Rumsfeld, Wolfowitz, et al.) are back hitting the federal sauce. George W has swigged so much that he's given America its first $2 trillion budget.

Admittedly, any recent president's budget is an exercise in political posturing and economic gimmickry, but this year's $2.4 trillion offering by George is a P. T. Barnum exercise in flimflam, economic voodoo, political whitewash, hog excrement, plutocratic pandering, and outright fraud.

Not only does Bush's budget not add up, it pretends that 2+2 equals 22 . . . and that you and I are too stupid to know the difference. Start with the fact that the Bushites admit that they have eaten all of the $240 billion surplus they inherited and will leave us with a $520 billion deficit in 2005 alone.

But the debt they're passing on to our children is far worse than that, for—*flimflam!*—Bush simply excluded from the budget any cost for his ongoing occupation of Iraq and Afghanistan, not to mention any cost for his war excursions into other evil-doing nations. He says he'll let us know how many gabillions these items will cost *after the November elections.*

If you went to a bank for a loan with numbers like these, not only would you be summarily rejected, but they'd haul your worthless carcass directly to debtor's prison!

The bulk of the debt that Bush is creating is not to cover things

> **" First and foremost, we got to make sure we fully fund LIHEAP,
> which is a way to help low-income folks, particularly here in the
> East, to pay for their high fuel bills. "**
>
> *—George W in 2000 campaign*
>
> (Bush's first budget slashed LIHEAP by 24.4 percent. His second budget cut
> it by another 21.4 percent.)

that strengthen our country and improve our lives, but merely to cover his giveaway of trillions of dollars from our public treasury to the corporations and millionaires who finance his presidency.

The Pentagon and its fraud-infested fat-cat contractors are awarded $400 billion—more than is budgeted for all the other agencies combined. Corporate Welfare is front and center, too. For example, polluters are given a pass on paying for the cleanup of Superfund sites—the nastiest, most contaminated spots in America. The Superfund law had taxed polluting industries to pay for cleaning up their own messes, but George W felt their pain and has now shifted the cost from the polluters to us pollutees, handing the tab to us taxpayers.

With these corporate giveaways, combined with his demand for even more tax givebacks to millionaires, the Bushites leave America's public larder bare for years to come. But this fits their plan perfectly, for now George is able to preach frugality, cut programs, and nix new ideas to benefit middle- and low-income people— you and me.

In March 2004, after having binged on budget Ripple for three solid years, a suddenly tightfisted Bush said without a trace of blush that lean times now require cuts in domestic spending: *"We're calling upon Congress to be wise with the taxpayers' money."*

Among his cuts:

Rural firefighter equipment
School dropout prevention
Work-training grants
Veterans health program
Emergency heating for low-income seniors
Preventing lead poisoning in children
EPA's clean-water fund
Nurse training
Prison rape prevention
College tuition grants
Modernizing the air-traffic-controller system
Local law enforcement assistance
After-school programs for children
Office of domestic preparedness
Modernizing the IRS to pursue corporate cheaters

Betrayal of Our Troops

If hypocrisy were a drug, Washington would be the crack capital of the world. Congressional and White House leaders these days seem to get up every morning and inject, smoke, snort, and otherwise mainline a doozy of a dose of hypocrisy to get them through their day.

On no issue is this addiction more obvious than in their treatment of America's ground soldiers and veterans. Politicians constantly bellow: "Support our troops!" They're particularly quick to hurl this red, white, and blue shout at any of us who dare question the motives and rationale for their bloody war in Iraq.

Most recently, Bush positioned himself as the soldier's president during his 2004 State of the Union speech, declaring, "Many of our troops are listening tonight. And I want you and your families to know . . . my administration, and this Congress, will give you the resources you need to fight and win the war on terror."

What a hypocrite! If you want to know how the Bushites "support our troops," check with any of the thousands of stunned military families who have learned that Bush's Pentagon has failed to provide essential equipment needed by our troops in Iraq and Afghanistan—everything from lifesaving body armor to warm gloves, from rifles that work to flashlights. The families, having received desperate calls, e-mails, and letters from the front lines, literally have had to go to their local stores, buy equipment, and ship it to their loved ones!

Yes, the same Pentagon that sops up $400 billion of our tax dollars every year (plus the $87 billion add-on it was given last year to pay for Bush's Iraqi occupation) is shamelessly shortchanging the grunts who are putting their lives on the line every day. The damning fact is that Bush and Congress, in their rah-rah rush to war, sent our men and women into the deadly fray without the proper equipment.

One of the important innovations for ground troops is a simple, relatively light vest that contains ceramic plates made of boron carbide capable of stopping powerful AK-47 bullets and flying shrapnel. Simply put, these vests are lifesavers in a firefight or an explosion. The vests were readily available to the Pentagon from U.S. manufacturers.

In 2002, the Pentagon spent $690 million just on *the cost overrun* charged by Lockheed-Martin for the F-22 jet fighter it is developing—a plane widely condemned as unneeded.

That same sum of money would have fully outfitted 87,000 ground troops from head to toe.

This is why Joe Werfelman was dismayed to hear from his son that he and other soldiers in Iraq did not have the vests. "He called us frantically three or four times on this," Werfelman told *The*

GET READY TO UPCHUCK

To plumb the depths of Bushite hypocrisy, check out their sickening treatment of seventeen American prisoners of war from the first Iraq war in 1991. These men were brutally tortured by Saddam's henchmen—punched, kicked, clubbed, burned, electrically shocked, starved, you name it. But they endured, returning home in '91, where they were welcomed by then–defense secretary Dick Cheney: "Your country is opening its arms to greet you," he gushed.

A decade later, the POWs found some measure of justice in a law that allowed them to sue the Iraqi government for the physical and psychological damage they had suffered, with payments to be made from frozen Iraqi assets that the ruling elites had stashed in foreign banks. In 2002, a judge ruled for the seventeen POWs, and last July he awarded them damages of nearly $1 billion.

Good! But wait. Only two weeks later, Bush's Justice Department asked to intervene in the POWs' case with the intention not merely of reversing the monetary reward but also of wiping the case from the books, as though the torture never happened!

Washington Post. Instead, the troops had been issued Vietnam-era flak jackets that, as one soldier put it, "couldn't stop a rock." So Werfelman scrambled, found a New Jersey company that makes the ceramic gear, paid $660, and shipped it off to Iraq. "If the army is not going to protect him, we've got to do it," says Joe.

Enraged military families later learned that even the small contingent of troops that Mongolia sent to help the U.S. in Iraq came with lifesaving vests. If Mongolia can do it, why not America, they asked? Hauled before a House committee, the head of U.S. forces in Iraq, General John Abizaid, said he could not "answer for the record why we started this war with protective vests that were in short supply."

Their rationale? They said that Bush had confiscated these frozen assets last March by executive order when he launched his war on Iraq, so therefore the money technically was no longer an Iraqi asset, but instead belonged to the U.S. government.

The White House said that, while it could choose to use the money to pay the POWs, it chose not to, claiming that it needed the money "for the urgent national security needs of *rebuilding Iraq.*" Now the attorney general is even appealing the judge's original ruling that held Iraq responsible for the torture, asserting that with Saddam gone, all U.S. sanctions against Iraq must be removed—apparently retroactively. One of the POWs, Jeff Fox, stated the obvious: "It sends a very bad message that a commander in chief would place veterans and prisoners of war second behind a foreign nation."

Asked last fall by CBS to comment, Dick Cheney's aide said he was "too busy." The White House that demands that all the rest of us "support our troops" has not even had a staffer—much less the president—give these seventeen POWs the courtesy of a phone call.

Thanks to the howl and heat from the grassroots, Congress added money to the Pentagon's already bloated budget last fall, requiring body armor for all soldiers in Iraq. Finally, nearly a year after Bush started his war, and after an untold number of unnecessary deaths, our troops are receiving the vests.

Pentagon budgeteers are quietly skimping on even the small stuff for our soldiers. A Houston father visited his marine son at Camp Pendleton a year ago, just before the son shipped out to Iraq. "I was shocked and outraged to hear the list of items the Marine Corps was *not* going to provide." The father rushed to a surplus store and bought $250 worth of essentials—mosquito netting, flashlight, canteen, undershirts, assorted hitches and straps, etc. "I was really taken aback," he says. "I was sure the military would support the troops in all the equipment they needed. How wrong I was."

It's not like the Pentagon, White House, and Congress were unaware before the Iraqi invasion that our ground troops would be ill-equipped. The same thing had happened in 2002 when the infantry was sent into Afghanistan to do the dirty work of going cave to cave, often under fire, in search of al Qaeda and Taliban forces. Families of the GIs created a mini shopping boom as they were forced to buy gloves, cushioned socks, cargo belts, flashlights, padded rucksack straps, hydration systems, satellite position-finders, and other basics to send to the troops—things the Pentagon did not provide.

Washington lavishes billions on fat-cat weapons-makers (whose sons and daughters mostly don't go to war), while it tells our troops on the ground to send their military shopping lists home to their families.

Who Gets Taxed?

You have to admire the compassionate conservatism of the only president we presently have. George W has looked around the country, surveyed the growing economic woes of our people, and reached the compassionate conclusion that the rich are hurting.

Feeling their pain, George responded last year with a $400 billion tax giveback for these privileged ones, eliminating the taxes they pay on their dividends or stock profits. But this is not merely a matter of compassion, says George, it's a matter of: justice.

The assertion by Bush is that taxing the stock dividends of big investors is nothing less than the horror of "double taxation." After all, claim the Bushites, corporations already pay taxes on these profits, so the 10 percent of Americans who own 90 percent of all corporate stock shouldn't pay again when the profits are distributed to them. George, who likes things simple, says simply, "It's not fair to tax something twice."

> **" If class warfare is being waged in America, my class is clearly winning. "**
> —*Billionaire investor Warren Buffett, who has consistently argued against Bush's tax giveaways to the rich*

Yoo-hoo . . . George . . . we know you've never worked for a living, but have none of your hotshot corporate economists mentioned to you that working people have their incomes taxed not just twice, but multiple times? Check it out: Our monthly wages are hit for federal and state income taxes, social security tax, unemployment and medicare taxes; then these same wages are slapped with ever-rising sales taxes, the gasoline tax, property taxes, highway and subway tolls, numerous fees . . . and if we buy a six-pack to try to forget taxes, we're hit with the liquor tax.

While we're taking hit after hit, the Bushites continue to allow corporations to take a hike on April 15. Here's a fairly new and ridiculous example of their many tax dodges: Corporations buy enormous amounts of product from abroad, listing these purchases and expenses as deductible from their income taxes. Only, the prices they pay are absurd, such as buying thousands of jars of salad dressing from Brazil at a price of $720 per jar, or buying loads of tweezers from Japan at $4,896 each.

What we have here is a massive money-laundering scheme in which corporations are "buying" supplies and services from their own overseas subsidiaries—that is, from themselves. By grossly inflating the price they pay, these phony purchases move huge sums of corporate profits out of our country into the accounts of their foreign affiliates, thus escaping U.S. taxation on those profits.

Scamming Uncle Sam has become very big business, according to two highly respected finance professors who've been tracking this annual rip-off for a decade. Simon Pak and John Zdanowicz calculate that this "transfer pricing," as they call it, cost our public treasury $53 billion last year alone, and it's on the rise. Wow, $53 billion would pay for a lot of health care, bridge and road repairs, alternative energy research, and other crying needs that the politicians keep telling us there's no money to finance!

Instead, this $53 billion was pocketed by the tax thieves. The transfers go two ways. In addition to buying from foreign subsidiaries, U.S. corporations also *sell* products to their overseas affiliates at ridiculously low prices, such as selling missile launchers to an Israeli subsidiary for $52 each.

This corporate fraud is blatant and easily detectable, *yet the Treasury Department doesn't even track these international tax-evading transactions, much less prosecute them.*

But the IRS is hot on the trail of another group. With full backing from Bush and the GOP's congressional leaders, the tax agency has launched a massive, bureaucratic, intrusive, wasteful, unfair, elitist, intimidating, mean, abusive, and just-plain-stupid effort to crack down on the meager tax filings of the working poor.

Their target is a successful program called the Earned Income Tax Credit. It's for people who work in low-wage jobs at McDonald's, Wal-Mart, Starbucks, and the like, offsetting some of the taxes these workers would pay and helping them to rise a bit above poverty. The average credit for workers with children is less than $2,000 a year, but that can make a difference when your job only pays $12,000 to $20,000 a year.

Some 4 million Americans count on this tax credit, but the Bushites now intend to harass them from using the program. They've issued new IRS rules that require recipients to submit documented proof that they are eligible *in advance* of claiming the tax credit. This is a cumbersome, complex, and intimidating burden of advance proof that is not required of corporations that have entire tax firms to hop them through loopholes and gain tax breaks not of a mere $2,000, but of $20 million, $200 million, or more.

The new rules are so severe that honest, low-income taxpayers now have to hire tax preparers to handle the extra paperwork—and meanwhile, George W has asked Congress for $100 million to hire hundreds of new IRS agents to go after these poor workers.

Let's Run Government Like A . . .

Here's a new political slogan with some integrity and democratic gravitas to it: "Let's run government like a government."

This is, of course, the opposite of the tired, old, tried-and-failed slogan that politicians of both parties have been pushing for years: "We'll run government like a business." The Clintonites used this in the nineties with their "reinventing government" campaign, declaring that government agencies should become efficient business operations and treat people as "customers."

Oh? Efficient like what?—the mammoth insurance-company bureaucracies, or maybe the military contractors who waste and defraud us of billions of our tax dollars? And do they mean customer treatment like we get from don't-give-a-damn banks and telephone companies?

Today we have a fully corporatized White House run by former CEOs. They're literally running government through such standard corporate practices as operating in secret, twisting tax laws to benefit the elite, opposing public disclosure and right-to-know laws, shutting out dissenters and dissing dissent itself, rigging the regulatory rules for corporate gain, stomping on labor, running roughshod over the environment, disempowering consumers, and using advertising gimmicks to hide their deceits.

It's time to get real. Government is not a business and we are not customers. We're *citizens!* Far from being passive consumers of government policies, we're the sovereign powers who can make or unmake those policies. Corporations, by their very nature, are exclusive private empires that exist to serve the bottom line of the wealthiest investors (including the CEOs), everyone and everything else be damned. That's no model for a democracy.

America's founders knew that corporate power was anathema to the public interest and the democratic will of the people, so they created a framework to run government like a government. It's time to put those democratic principles into action again.

Heroes

The great strength of America is not in corporate chieftains and presidents, but in rank-and-file folks who give a damn not only about themselves and their own family's fortunes but also about the larger community and doing what's right. Despite the current practices of Washington and Wall Street, which embrace a self-serving ethic of "Get yours" and "Get away with as much as you can," the prevailing ethic that built our nation and still unifies it today is: "We're all in this together."

To "promote the general welfare" is one of six founding purposes of our governing system, as expressed in the first sentence of the Constitution of the United States of America. That's just the spirit of the common good, and it abounds yet all across our land. We need to touch that spirit more and build a new politics that dares to call it forth from all of us so that America might in fact be governed by it.

I find this spirit wherever I go, and I've even seen it in the unlikeliest of places: Congress! It's been said that occasionally "an innocent man" gets sent to the legislature, and Bob Eckhardt was one such man.

Bob wasn't innocent in the biblical sense, for he was way too earthy and worldly for that. Nor was he at all innocent in the sense of being simple or naive, for he was awfully smart and a crafty legislator to boot. But Bob *was* innocent in the sense of being honest, without guile—the very kind of fellow you'd hope to find in a legislature representing you. Now he's gone, having slipped his earthly traces in 2002 at the ripe age of eighty-eight, but having enjoyed his rich life right to the end.

What a character. A labor lawyer, whiskey drinker, storyteller, state legislator, and member of Congress, Bob was the exact opposite of today's poll-driven, money-grubbing, blow-dried politicians. He was given to wearing rumpled white linen suits and red bowties, he rode a bicycle to his Capitol Hill office, he liked to write and sleep in tree houses he would build behind wherever he lived, he had a drawl that could melt a block of ice and a mind that could slice and dice a whole roomful of Gucci-clad corporate lobbyists sent in to slick the slow talker from Houston.

What a loss. Eckhardt was an unabashed, unequivocating champion of working families, the environment, poor people, minorities, and underdogs in general. He never wavered, never sold out, never quit battling. Years ago someone accosted Bob's mother, saying that her son shouldn't be standing up so much for black people. "Oh, I'm afraid that's my fault," she retorted. "I raised him to be a Christian." Bob was an extraordinary treasure, not only because he consistently stood on principle during all of his years in public office, but also because he had a genius for translating principle into laws that actually helped ordinary folks. From the Clean Air Act to Open Beaches, from wage laws to the War Powers Act, Bob Eckhardt was a fighter for the common good.

Most such folks, however, are way outside of the halls of power, whether governmental or corporate, and there are many who rank as American heroes.

Not the fantasy superheroes depicted in action movies, but real-life workaday Americans who risk their careers and reputations to take a principled stand for what's right.

Time magazine honored three of these folks as its "People of the Year" for 2002. One was Sherron Watkins, the mid-level Enron executive who dared to confront her top boss about the gross corruption running rampant in this avaricious corporation; second was Coleen Rowley, the FBI field agent who blew the whistle on the agency's top brass for preventing her and other field staff from pursuing the September 11 terrorists *before* they struck; and third was Cynthia Cooper, WorldCom's internal auditor who went to the board of directors with the startling discovery that top executives had engineered $4 billion in financial "irregularities."

The extraordinary thing about these three women is that their heroism is not all that extraordinary. It rarely gets much media play, and it sure doesn't always topple the mighty, but every day in our country there are principled people standing up to their unprincipled higher-ups . . . and often paying the price.

David Mihalic, for example, is a thirty-three-year park service veteran who was recently forced out of the job he cherished because he would not go along with his political bosses and the White House, who wanted to let developers ram a highway through the Great Smoky Mountains National Park. "What we do here," Mihalic said of the park service, "we have to do for the common good."

Eduardo Delacruz, a New York City police officer, is another example. Just before Christmas he was suspended without pay because he refused to arrest a homeless man found sleeping in a garage. When ordered to make the arrest, Delacruz still refused, saying the man had nowhere to go and it was simply wrong to put him in jail for that.

Heroism is not glamorous, it's gutsy, egalitarian . . . and way more American than George W. Bush and that crowd.

BUSHFLIPS

Draw a line from George W's statements in the column on the left to match them with his subsequent statement or actions in the column on the right.

What Bush Said

1. "The most important thing is for us to find Osama bin Laden."

2. "I'm a uniter, not a divider."

3. "We're dealing with first-time responders to make sure they've got what's needed to be able to respond."

4. "I'm working with Congress to make sure they hear the message—the message of fiscal responsibility."

5. "Our veterans from every era are the finest of citizens. We owe them the life we know today."

6. "With the support of Congress, we will work to provide the resources schools need to fund the era of reform."

7. "For diplomacy to be effective, words must be credible—and no one can now doubt the word of America."

8. "We've got to do more to protect worker pensions."

9. "I hope people around this country realize that agencies such as this food bank need money. They need our contributions."

10. Bush says the "Mission Accomplished" banner on the deck of the USS *Lincoln* was placed there by sailors.

What He Did

A. Tried to cut more than $1 billion out of existing grants to local police and fire departments.

B. Admitted that intelligence on Iraqi WMDs was flawed, contrary to public statements made in the State of the Union address.

C. Proposed a 2005 budget that would put the government more than $520 billion into deficit.

D. Created the most polarized American political climate in recent memory.

E. Launched Operation Iraqi Freedom, diverting U.S. forces away from search for bin Laden.

F. Froze the Congregate Nutrition Program, which assists local soup kitchens and meals-on-wheels programs, cutting at least 36,000 seniors from meals-on-wheels.

G. Quietly admitted "Mission Accomplished" banner was placed there by his advance team.

H. After signing the No Child Left Behind Act, proposed $7 billion less than what was authorized under the bill.

I. Refused a $30 billion budget request for the VA to maintain its current level of services, leaving the agency nearly $4 billion short.

J. Bush's Treasury Department proposed new rules that would allow employers to resume converting traditional pension plans to new "cash balance" plans that can lower benefits to long-serving workers.

Answers on page 227.

You Name It!

☞ *The environment, the economy, foreign policy, the Pentagon, religion, taxes, judgeships, globalization, wealth, the sanctity of marriage, police power, the budget, global empire, executive authority ... you name it. In every area, Bush & Company are remaking America for us, making it right!*

What else can I say, amigos? The Eagle is soaring! With W, we've got us a national CEO who understands what it takes to be president and is willing to, you know, do what's got to be done. He and his boys (Dick, Donnie, Johnny, Condi, and Karl) know how to run this old world without letting anyone get in their way—not other countries, not Congress, not the courts, not Democrats (damned sure not them), not the Nosy Parker press, not public opinion, not the voters, not nobody.

George himself said it best (what an articulate guy he is, despite the derision of the liberal media): "I'm the commander, see. I do not need to explain why I say things. That's the interesting thing about being the president. Maybe somebody needs to explain to me why they say something, but I don't feel like I owe anybody an explanation."

The Big Stick is back! We shouldn't be surprised. George let everyone know what was coming back in November–December 2000 in that little Florida flare-up. While those sorry-assed Democrats pissed and moaned, Bush's bold team went to Florida and took things into their own strong hands. The Democrats are still whining about the whupping they took—"Oh, it's not fair. . . . Gore really won. . . .Those poor voters in Florida got stiffed. . . .You cheated. . . . Oh, woe is us"—and here's the one I just hate every time I hear it: "Bush isn't a legitimate president because he wasn't elected."

Wasn't elected? Hey, you bunch of squawking, bug-eyed roosters, what do you call that 5–4 vote on the Supreme Court? Wasn't that an election? And you lost, so here's my final word for you soreheads: Get over it!

Oh, and one more thing, who's sitting in the Oval Office right now, huh? There's all the proof you need, right there, about who "won."

America needs a strongman. And if you're not already behind the strongman in the White House today—a man strong enough to snatch victory from the Floridian jaws of defeat, strong enough to kick Saddam's fat butt using the full force of U.S. military might, strong enough to tell the U.N. and the French and those other pantywaist international types to lump it, strong enough to do all the things we've been talking about here—then, just maybe, you're not strong enough for the New America that's coming in term two.

I'll tell you what I'm thinking, and this might surprise you: term three. And four! Maybe more. Hell, George is not that old. Could go forever. What's with this Twenty-second Amendment, anyway? It's out of date. It was about stopping another FDR from grabbing more than two terms, but Bulletin, Folks: *We haven't had a lot of FDRs running lately.*

Why let this thing stand in George's way? He's 180 degrees op-posite of FDR. We've got a thoroughbred here, and it's stupid just to run him twice. I double-damn guarantee you that if we put him in for a second term, Karl and the boys will toss that two-term limit and turn W loose for posterity's sake.

But enough of me talking about why we have to elect George W. Bush. Let's hear you talk about it. Tell us what George W means to you. Some people tell me that words fail them when it comes to expressing exactly how passionate they feel about all the things that George has been doing, and one fellow even said he'd need a dictionary and a thesaurus to find just the right words to express the true depth of his feelings on all the Bush stuff he's seen. Also, I've gotta tell you that it nearly brought tears to my eyes when a young woman (a Democrat, too!) said to me that she considered George W to be the best Republican president since his daddy. Now how about that?

Like I said, though, it's your turn. What is it about Bush that has made the most incredible impression on you? Maybe it's one of his personal characteristics, or one of his many stunning initia-tives, or perhaps you've been struck by one of his profound state-ments or by some particularly amazing aspect of his philosophy of life.

Whatever it is about George that is motivating you to go to the polls this year, get it off your chest right here. Our fine publisher has generously provided space for you to add your own reason to the litany of "Perfectly Good Reasons to Elect George W. Bush," and Hightower welcomes your input and insights for his future works. Feel free to send your contribution to him, or if you prefer, you can send it directly to the Republican National Committee for its edification and thoughtful consideration!

WHAT GEORGE W MEANS TO ME

Jim Hightower
c/o Viking
375 Hudson Street, 4th Floor
New York, NY 10014
info@jimhightower.com

Republican National Committee
310 First Street, SE
Washington, DC 20003
www.gop.com

Clip and send!

CONNECTIONS

I'm often asked: "Where in the world do you get the information for all that stuff you write—do you just make it up, or are there actually sources for it?"

Indeed, there are sources. Ample of them, and legitimate to boot. On the one hand are the "Big E" Establishment sources, such as the *New York Times, BusinessWeek,* the *Wall Street Journal,* yada yada yada, which in unguarded back-page moments occasionally reveal corporate and governmental tidbits, quotes, rationalizations, insider facts, and candid confessions. We read those back pages, digest, and regurgitate.

But, best of all, is the virtually untapped treasure trove of public-interest, grassroots, advocacy, and other groups that cover every issue you could care about, covering each in depth, in breadth, and sometimes with insouciance (pardon my French). These groups, with their extensive analyses and assertive Web sites, pierce the thick shields of corporate and governmental propaganda, lay bare the deceit, and lay out the possibilities for reform. These groups form the deep veins of investigative gold that we mine—and you can, too. Here are but a few of them that we've used for the issues raised in this book. If there are credible sources you know about that we should add, please send them to us:

info@jimhightower.com.

217

ACORN
88 Third Avenue
Brooklyn, NY 11217
718-246-7900
www.acorn.org

AFL-CIO
815 16th Street, NW
Washington, DC 20006
202-637-5000
www.aflcio.org

Alternative Radio
P.O. Box 551
Boulder, CO 80306
800-444-1977
www.alternativeradio.org

AlterNet.org
77 Federal Street
San Francisco, CA 94107
415-284-1420
www.alternet.org

American Civil Liberties Union
125 Broad Street, 18th floor
New York, NY 10004
212-549-2585
www.aclu.org

American Library Association
50 East Huron
Chicago, IL 60611
800-545-2433
www.ala.org

Animal Welfare Institute
P.O. Box 3650
Washington, DC 20027
703-836-4300
www.awionline.org

Apollo Alliance
Bracken Hendricks, Director,
    New Growth Initiative
Institute for America's Future
1025 Connecticut Avenue, Suite
    205
Washington, DC 20036
202-955-5665
www.apolloalliance.org

Appalachian Center for the
    Economy and the
    Environment
P.O. Box 507
Lewisburg, WV 24901
304-645-9006
www.appalachian-center.org

Bill of Rights Defense
    Committee
241 King Street, Suite 216
Northampton, MA 01060
413-582-0110
www.bordc.org

Business Leaders for Sensible
    Priorities
P.O. Box 1976
Old Chelsea Station
New York, NY 10113
212-243-3146
www.sensiblepriorities.org

CalPERS
Lincoln Plaza
400 P Street
Sacramento, CA 95814
916-326-3991
www.calpers.ca.gov

Campaign for America's Future
1025 Connecticut Avenue, NW,
 Suite 205
Washington, DC 20036
202-955-5665
www.ourfuture.org

Campaign to Label Genetically
 Engineered Foods
P.O. Box 55699
Seattle, WA 98155
425-771-4049
www.thecampaign.org

Center for Budget & Policy
 Priorities
820 First Street, NE, Suite 510
Washington, DC 20002
202-408-1080
www.cbpp.org

Center for Democracy &
 Technology
1634 I Street, NW, Suite 1100
Washington, DC 20006
202-637-9800
www.cdt.org

Center for Digital Democracy
1718 Connecticut Avenue, NW,
 Suite 200
Washington, DC 20009
202-986-2220
www.democraticmedia.org

Center for Health, Environment,
 and Justice
P.O. Box 6806
Falls Church, VA 22040
703-237-2249
www.chej.org

Center for Responsive Politics
1101 14th Street, NW,
 Suite 1030
Washington, DC 20005-5635
202-857-0044
www.opensecrets.org

Center for Science in the Public
 Interest
1875 Connecticut Avenue, NW,
 Suite 300
Washington, DC 20009-5728
202-332-9110
www.cspinet.org

Citizens for Tax Justice
1311 L Street, NW
Washington, DC 20005
202-626-3780
www.ctj.org

Citizens Trade Campaign
P.O. Box 77077
Washington, DC 20013
202-778-3320
www.citizenstrade.org

Commercial Alert
4110 SE Hawthorne Boulevard,
 #123
Portland, OR 97214-5426
503-235-8012
www.commercialalert.org

Common Cause
1250 Connecticut Avenue, NW,
 #600
Washington, DC 20036
202-833-1200
www.commoncause.org

Communications Workers of
America
501 3rd Street, NW
Washington, DC 20001-2797
202-434-1168
www.cwa-union.org

Conscious Choice
920 Franklin Street, #202
Chicago, IL 60610
312-440-4373
www.consciouschoice.com

Council of Institutional
Investors
1730 Rhode Island Avenue,
Suite 512
Washington, DC 20036
202-822-0800
www.cii.org

Debs-Jones-Douglass Institute
1532 16th Street, NW
Washington, DC 20036
202-234-0040
www.djdinstitute.org

Democracy Now!
DCTV
P.O. Box 693
New York, NY 10013
212-431-9090
www.democracynow.org

Democracy 21
1825 I Street, NW, Suite 400
Washington, DC 20006
202-429-2008
www.democracy21.org

Disabled American Veterans
3725 Alexandria Pike
Cold Spring, KY 41076
859-441-7300
www.dav.org

Doctors Without Borders
333 Seventh Avenue, 2nd Floor
New York, NY 10001-5004
212-679-6800
www.doctorswithoutborders.org

Earthworks
1612 K Street, NW, Suite 808
Washington, DC 20006
202-887-1872
www.mineralpolicy.org

Economic Policy Institute
1600 L Street, NW, Suite 1200
Washington, DC 20036
202-775-8810
www.epinet.org

Ecopledge
29 Temple Place, Suite 200
Boston, MA 02111
617-747-4347
www.ecopledge.com

Electronic Privacy Information
Center (EPIC)
1718 Connecticut Avenue, NW,
Suite 200
Washington, DC 20009
202-483-1140
www.epic.org

Environmental Working Group
1436 U Street, NW, Suite 100
Washington, DC 20009
202-667-6982
www.ewg.org

Fairness and Accuracy in
    Reporting (FAIR)
112 West 27th Street
New York, NY 10001
212-633-6700
www.fair.org

Families USA
1334 G Street, NW
Washington, DC 20005
202-628-3030
www.familiesusa.org

Federation of American
    Scientists
1717 K Street, NW, Suite 209
Washington, DC 20036
202-546-3300
www.fas.org

Free Speech TV
P.O. Box 6060
Boulder, CO 80306
303-442-8445
www.freespeech.org

Friends of the Earth
1717 Massachusetts Avenue,
    NW, Suite 600
Washington, DC 20036-2002
877-843-8687
www.foe.org

Global Exchange
2017 Mission Street, #303
San Francisco, CA 94110
415-255-7296
www.globalexchange.org

Global Trade Watch
215 Pennsylvania Avenue, SE
Washington, DC 20003
202-546-4996
www.tradewatch.org

GRACE Factory Farm Project
    (Global Resource Action
    Center for the Environment)
215 Lexington Avenue,
    Suite 1001
New York, NY 10016
212-726-9161
www.factoryfarm.org

Greenpeace USA
702 H Street, NW, Suite 300
Washington, DC 20001
202-462-1177
www.greenpeaceusa.org

Heritage Forest Campaign
1200 18th Street, NW, 5th Floor
Washington, DC 20036
202-887-8800
www.ourforests.org

Institute for Global Ethics
11 Main Street
P.O. Box 563
Camden, ME 04843
207-236-6658
www.globalethics.org

In These Times
2040 North Milwaukee Avenue
Chicago, IL 60647
773-772-0100
www.inthesetimes.org

Local Harvest
831-475-8150
www.localharvest.org

Military Families Speak Out
www.mfso.org

Mother Jones Magazine
731 Market Street, 6th floor
San Francisco, CA 94103
415-665-6637
www.motherjones.com

Multinational Monitor
P.O. Box 19405
Washington, DC 20036
202-387-8034
http://multinationalmonitor.org

The Nation
33 Irving Place
New York, NY 10003
212-209-5400
www.thenation.com

National Academy of Sciences
500 Fifth Street, NW
Washington, DC 20001
202-334-2000
www.nas.edu

National Parks Conservation
   Association
1300 19th Street, NW, Suite
   300
Washington, DC 20036
800-628-7275
www.npca.org

National Priorities Project
17 New South Street, Suite 302
Northampton, MA 01060
413-584-9556
www.nationalpriorities.org

National Wildlife Federation
11100 Wildlife Center Drive
Reston, VA 20190-5362
800-822-9919
www.nwf.org

Natural Resources Defense
   Council
40 West 20th Street
New York, NY 10011
212-727-2700
www.nrdc.org

New Dimensions Radio
P.O. Box 569
Ukiah, CA 95482
707-468-5215
www.newdimensions.org

NORML (National
   Organization for the Reform
   of Marijuana Laws)
1600 K Street, NW, Suite 501
Washington, DC 20006-2832
202-483-5500
www.norml.org

North American Industrial
   Hemp Council
P.O. Box 259329
Madison, WI 53725-9329
www.naihc.org

Nuclear Information and
   Resource Service
World Information Service on
   Energy
1424 16th Street, NW, #404
Washington, DC 20036
202-328-0002
www.nirs.org

Organic Consumers Association
6101 Cliff Estate Road
Little Marais, MN 55614
218-226-4164
www.organicconsumers.org

Physicians for a National Health
   Program
29 East Madison, Suite 602
Chicago, IL 60602
312-782-6006
www.pnhp.org

Primavera Foundation
702 South Sixth Avenue
Tucson, AZ 85701
520-623-5111
www.primavera.org

The Progressive
409 East Main Street
Madison, WI 53703
608-257-4626
www.progressive.org

Progressive Populist
P.O. Box 150517
Austin, TX 78715-0517
512-447-0455
www.populist.com

Public Citizen
1600 20th Street, NW
Washington, DC 20009
202-588-1000
www.citizen.org

Public Interest Research Group
Higher Education Project
218 D Street, SE
Washington, DC 20003
202-546-9707
www.pirg.org/highered

Safe Energy Communication
   Council
1717 Massachusetts Avenue,
   NW, Suite 805
Washington, DC 20036
202-483-8491
www.safeenergy.org

Silicon Valley Toxics Coalition
760 North First Street
San Jose, CA 95112
408-287-6707
www.svtc.org

Sojourners
2401 15th Street, NW
Washington, DC 20009
202-328-8842
www.sojo.net

The Lands Council
423 West First Avenue, Suite 240
Spokane, WA 99201
509-838-4912
www.landscouncil.org

TomPaine.com
1636 Connecticut Avenue, NW,
    Suite 30
Washington, DC 20009
202-332-2881
www.tompaine.com

Trial Lawyers for Public Justice
1717 Massachusetts Avenue,
    NW, Suite 800
Washington, DC 20036
202-797-8600
www.tlpj.org

U.S. Public Interest
Research Group
218 D Street, SE
Washington, DC 20003
202-546-9707
www.uspirg.org

Utne Magazine
1624 Harmon Place
Minneapolis, MN 55403
612-338-5040
www.utne.com

SOLUTIONS TO PUZZLES

Solution to BushWord Puzzle (page 38)

Answers to BushQuiz (page 73)

1. C	6. D
2. D	7. C
3. D	8. D
4. D	9. C
5. D	10. D

Solution to BushFind (page 114)

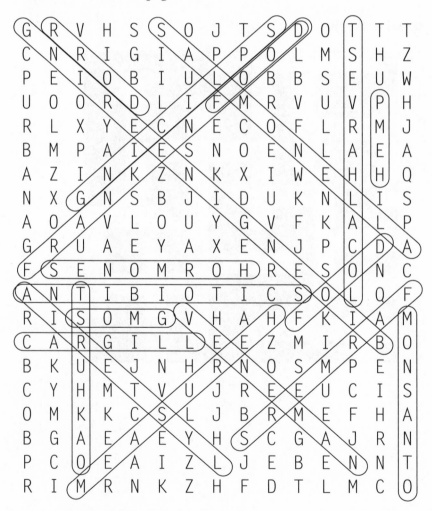

Answers to BushScramble (page 153)

1. ASHCROFT
2. PRIVACY
3. GEORGE W
4. RANCHETTE
5. MADISON
6. FREE SPEECH
7. CIVIL LIBERTIES
8. HOMELAND SECURITY
9. ORWELL
10. OPERATION PIPE DREAMS

Answers to BushFlips (page 209)

1. E	6. H
2. D	7. B
3. A	8. J
4. C	9. F
5. I	10. G

INDEX